Part 1

Whispers from Home

Chapter 1

I was born in the beautiful islands of Fiji in 1965—a place where life mirrored the ocean that surrounded us: serene on the surface, but often stormy underneath. My early years were shaped by a harsh reality that struck far too soon. My parents' divorce shattered the sense of warmth, stability, and family I might have known. They separated when I was very young, and with my mother pregnant with my sister and unable to care for me, I was placed in the care of my grandparents.

Eventually, I was entrusted to my mother's sister and her husband, who took on the responsibility of raising me. Though it was a gesture of duty, it was also the beginning of a life where I often felt like I didn't belong.

In many ways, my story mirrors the tale of Cinderella—only without the magic. Hardships and sorrow cast long shadows over my young heart. Like her, I longed for a childhood filled with laughter and light, for the joy and freedom that every child deserves. But instead of fairytales, I lived in a world of responsibility—one where I had to grow up far too fast.

There were no fairy godmothers in my story, no glass slippers or enchanted moments to whisk me away. There was only me—alone with my thoughts, learning how to survive. I had to find strength within myself, to rise each day and face a life that demanded more from me than it ever should have. And somehow, through the pain and struggle, I discovered a quiet resilience that would later become my greatest ally.

My childhood was not made of play, but of work and duty. I had responsibilities far beyond my years. Mornings began not with cartoons or carefree chatter, but with chores—cooking, cleaning, washing, caring for others. These tasks were not occasional help or small favors—they were daily expectations, and I met them without question.

There were days when it all felt too heavy, like I was carrying an invisible weight no one else could see. While other children played freely outdoors, I remained behind closed doors, scrubbing, sweeping, doing whatever was needed to keep the household running.

Growing up in that environment forced me to mature quickly. Though it gave me strength and resourcefulness, it also left a deep, aching void—the absence of a childhood I could never reclaim. I yearned for simple joys, for love that didn't come with conditions, for moments that felt truly mine.

I adored the idea of family, yet I couldn't bring myself to embrace my own. Somewhere along the way, bitterness took root—a quiet resentment toward those who had stolen what should have been the most innocent, joyful time of my life.

Over time, those early experiences became the silent lessons I carried with me. They molded me into someone who could weather life's storms with quiet determination. But even strength has its shadows. Beneath the resilience was a gap that no amount of endurance could truly fill—a hollow space where affection, comfort, and a sense of belonging should have lived.

I longed for the closeness of family—the kind of easy laughter and shared warmth that fills a home with safety and love. I dreamed of arms that wrapped around me not out of obligation, but because I was cherished. But that kind of comfort remained just out of reach.

Still, in those quiet, solitary moments—folding clothes, preparing meals, sweeping floors—I discovered tiny fragments of strength buried deep inside me. They weren't loud or grand, but they were mine. And they mattered. That quiet strength became my anchor, something steady I could hold on to when the world around me felt uncertain.

It was that inner strength that carried me forward. It allowed me to endure the weight of abandonment, the ache of unspoken grief, and the sting of dreams that had to be tucked away too soon. My childhood wasn't filled with magic, but it gave me something else: the will to keep going, to hope, to someday build the life I never had.

Supporting myself mentally, physically, and emotionally became more than just a routine—it became my mantra, my survival strategy in a world that often felt indifferent to my pain. There was no safety net, no shoulder to cry on when the weight of life became too much. I had to be my own source of strength—not because I felt ready, but because I had no other choice.

The strength I drew on didn't come from confidence; it came from necessity. Every challenge I faced demanded a kind of courage I hadn't yet discovered in myself. But slowly, step by step, I learned how to rise.

My journey is one of perseverance—of learning not only to endure hardship but to grow through it. I began to understand that my story wasn't only about surviving—it was about transforming pain into power. And in sharing it, I hold onto the hope that someone, somewhere, might read these words and see a reflection of their own struggle. That they too might find the strength to keep going, to believe that rising is possible—no matter how deep the fall.

Chapter 2:

After finishing grade 10, my dreams of continuing school faded into the background, overshadowed by the urgent need to support myself. Education had to wait—if it would ever return at all. I was sixteen, and childhood had officially ended.

I never had a birthday celebration growing up. Not once. Not the kind other kids got—cake, candles, laughter, or even a simple "Happy Birthday" that felt like it meant something. Every year, I held onto a tiny thread of hope that maybe this year would be different. That someone—anyone—would remember and make it special. Because birthdays matter to a child. They're supposed to be magical. A day to feel seen, celebrated, loved.

It wasn't until I turned sixteen that I experienced my very first birthday celebration. My mother organized it. There was cake, people, and for the first time, I felt what it meant to be noticed on that one special day. But even then, the joy was laced with the heaviness of all the years that had passed without it. Sixteen birthdays had come and gone in silence. That one celebration couldn't erase the loneliness of the others—but it did leave a small mark of warmth in a childhood that had known so little.

Sixteen should have been sweet. A milestone. But for me, it was a marker of something else entirely: survival. The moment when I stopped waiting for anyone to show up for me and realized I'd have to show up for myself.

With no time to hesitate, I stepped into a world shaped by adult responsibilities. My first job was as a receptionist at a doctor's surgery—a modest role, but to me, it was a triumph. I remember how proud I felt when I got the job. I had earned my place, and with that small victory came a sense of dignity that was entirely my own.

I worked five days a week, with Saturdays as half-days, and received twenty dollars each week. That modest paycheck may seem small by the world's standards, but to me, it was everything. It represented independence, purpose, and proof that I could stand on my own two feet.

But the reality of working life wasn't without its emotional costs. While my peers and siblings continued their studies and spent their days in the rhythms of adolescence, I was already living in a different world. I felt a growing distance from my siblings—an unspoken gap shaped by our differing experiences. We were bound by blood, but our lives were no longer walking the same path.

There was a moment—just before everything shifted—when I almost left Fiji entirely, not for Australia, but for America. I had been living with my aunt and uncle until I was sixteen. They had made the decision to migrate to the United States and, before they left, they offered to adopt me and take me with them. On the surface, it sounded like an opportunity. A new country. A new life. They even went to a solicitor and arranged all the necessary documents. All that was needed was my mother's signature.

But she refused to sign.

At the time, I didn't understand it. I thought it was just another instance of her keeping something good from me. Another barrier. Another rejection. But now, looking back, I see it differently. I wasn't being rescued—I was being recruited. If I had gone with them, I wouldn't have been their daughter. I would have been their housemaid. Again.

It's just as well she didn't sign. I might have ended up in another version of captivity—across the ocean, but no freer than before.

Yet, in the quiet of my days, there was one steady presence: my grandmother. Our bond grew deeper during this time, becoming a quiet refuge from the weight of the world outside. I cared for her with a tenderness that came naturally, and in return, she gave me something priceless—a sense of being seen, of being loved.

She was my anchor in a time when everything else felt uncertain. Our shared moments were simple—cups of tea, quiet conversations, silent companionship—but they were golden. They reminded me that even in the hardest seasons, love could still live in the quiet corners of everyday life.

Amidst the many challenges life threw at me, I held tight to a quiet dream—a vision of a better life, a fresh start far beyond the shores of Fiji. I imagined a future where I could feel free, where I could live life on my own terms, surrounded by peace and purpose. That vision of something brighter sustained me through even the darkest moments.

Eventually, I took a leap of faith. I left behind the only life I had known—with all its pain, memories, and complexity—and stepped into the unknown with nothing but courage and hope in my heart.

Australia represented a new beginning. A land of unfamiliar faces and uncertain paths, but also one full of possibility. Here, I had a chance to rediscover myself—to write my own story, not one written for me by circumstances or the past.

At first, life in Australia was overwhelming. I faced culture shock, loneliness, and the quiet ache of displacement. The customs were unfamiliar, the way of life so different from what I had known. I often felt like an outsider, navigating a world that didn't quite understand me. But I was determined to adapt, to grow, to find my place.

I learned to embrace the differences instead of resisting them. I allowed each challenge to teach me something new—about people, about the world, and most importantly, about myself. I worked hard to create a life of stability and meaning. Slowly, I began to carve out a sense of home—not from bricks and walls, but from resilience, learning, and self-worth.

This chapter of my life wasn't just about change—it was about reclaiming my power. It was the beginning of becoming the woman I was always meant to be.

Part 2:
Lost Love

Chapter 3:

I'll never forget the day I met Stuart, the first love of my life. After exchanging letters for 12 precious months, Stuart and I poured our hearts out to each other as pen pals. With every email, we'd share snippets of our lives - cherished photos, whispered dreams, and deepest hopes. As the days turned into weeks, and weeks into months, our words wove a tapestry of connection that felt almost sacred. Though miles apart, our bond grew stronger with each passing day, filling the spaces between our messages with laughter, understanding, and a sense of belonging.

The moment I stepped off the plane at Cairns Airport, time seemed to slow. There he was—Stuart—waiting just beyond the arrivals gate, a gentle smile on his face, looking effortlessly handsome in his neatly pressed shorts, crisp shirt, and knee-high socks. His presence felt like something out of a dream, familiar and yet breathtakingly new. As I approached, his cup of coffee trembled slightly in his hand, a subtle sign of the nerves he tried to hide. But when our eyes met, all uncertainty melted away. I felt an instant, inexplicable sense of comfort, like I had just found something I didn't even know I was missing.

He was tall, with a slender frame that seemed to stretch toward the sky, and I couldn't help but notice how small I felt standing before him. Yet rather than feeling overshadowed, I felt cherished. That contrast—his height against my petite frame—only added to the sense of wonder swirling around us.

Our first hug felt like coming home. And then came the kiss—a soft, tender meeting of lips that carried all the sweetness of possibility. It wasn't just a kiss; it was a quiet promise, a spark of something real and rare. In that fleeting moment, something shifted, like the universe had tilted slightly to bring us together.

I was 21, full of carefree hope and dreams I hadn't yet named. Stuart was 24, just a few steps ahead in life, with a quiet confidence and youthful charm that drew me in effortlessly. The difference in age didn't matter; from the moment we met, we moved in sync, as if our souls had already agreed on something our minds hadn't yet caught up to. I didn't know where this journey would lead, but in that magical first encounter, I knew my life had just changed—forever.

Vroom!! Stuart and I cruised through the streets of Cairns in his sleek red Commodore, the engine purring like a promise of something new. The wind played with my hair, and I couldn't help but smile—this wasn't just a ride to his family's home; it was the start of something real, something beautiful. The car, bold and bright like Stuart himself, mirrored the rush of emotions in my chest.

As we pulled into the driveway, my heart beat a little faster. I was about to meet the people who raised the man I had fallen so quickly—and so deeply—for. He lived with his mum, his sister, and two brothers, and from the moment I stepped through the door, they welcomed me like I'd always belonged. There was no awkwardness, no hesitation—just warmth, laughter, and an ease that wrapped around me like a soft blanket. I felt like I was already part of the crew.

Leaving my family behind in Fiji had left a quiet ache in my heart. But here, with Stuart's family in Australia, that ache began to soften. I wasn't losing a family—I was gaining another. Their kindness and love filled the empty spaces, and slowly, I began to feel whole again.

Stuart's mum had prepared a room just for me. It was small and cozy, with a sweet card on the bedside table and fresh flowers that filled the air with the scent of home. That simple gesture touched me deeply. She didn't just make space for me in her house—she made space for me in her heart. She respected my need for privacy, never once making me feel like a guest. Over time, she became like a second mother to me, someone I could trust and turn to. Calling her "Mum" came naturally—an unspoken promise of love and respect that grew between us day by day

Stuart and I were taking things slow, letting our love unfold naturally, like a sunrise—steady, warm, and full of promise. On my first night at his family home, after a lovely dinner filled with laughter and stories, we stepped outside to soak in the quiet of the evening. The sky was painted in deep shades of indigo, with stars beginning to peek through like tiny promises above us.

We sat close together, the night air cool against our skin, the soft rustle of leaves whispering around us. There was a stillness in the air, a kind of magic that made everything feel suspended in time. Stuart reached for my hand, and I felt the warmth of his palm wrap around mine, grounding me.

Then, in one gentle motion, he rose and knelt down in front of me. My breath caught. His eyes, filled with sincerity and something deeper—something eternal—met mine, and in that moment, it felt like the universe had gone quiet, waiting.

"I love you," he said, voice steady but thick with emotion. "You've brought a kind of light into my life I didn't know was missing. Will you marry me?"

No ring. No grand spectacle. Just the man I loved, offering his heart under a sky full of stars. And in that still, breathtaking moment, I knew—he was the one.

Tears welled in my eyes as I whispered "Yes," my voice trembling with joy. I threw my arms around him, laughter and happy tears mingling as we held each other beneath the open sky. It was perfect—quiet, sincere, and overflowing with love.

When word of the proposal spread, it was as if the whole house lit up with joy. Mum sprang into action, her excitement contagious as she imagined an intimate backyard wedding filled with charm and love.

She envisioned soft lights strung through the trees, delicate flowers swaying in the breeze, and close family gathered in the lush garden where love already bloomed so naturally. The thought of exchanging vows surrounded by nature's beauty, with the people who meant the most to us, made my heart soar.

As plans began to take shape, I often caught myself daydreaming about that day—our day—and felt an overwhelming sense of gratitude. For the love I had found, the family I had gained, and the quiet magic of that starry night when everything changed.

Chapter 4:

It felt like the entire world paused for a moment. I remember waking up with a strange feeling in my body—tired, a little dizzy, and more emotional than usual. Something was different, though I couldn't quite put my finger on it.

A few days passed with that nagging suspicion in the back of my mind. My period was late, but I didn't want to jump to conclusions. Still, curiosity and hope tugged at me, so I found myself standing in the pharmacy aisle, heart pounding, staring at a row of pregnancy tests. I picked one up with trembling hands, not sure whether to feel terrified or thrilled.

Back home, I took the test and sat in silence, eyes fixed on the little window. When the two lines appeared—clear and unmistakable—my breath caught in my throat. I was pregnant. A smile slowly crept across my face, and then came the tears—tears of joy, disbelief, and overwhelming gratitude.

I placed a hand on my belly, even though it was still flat, still untouched by the changes to come. "Hello, little one," I whispered. "I can't believe you're really here."

It was a feeling like no other—the mix of excitement and nervous anticipation, the wonder of knowing that a tiny life had begun inside me. I was going to be a mother. And in that instant, everything changed. The world felt brighter, the future more vivid, and my heart so full it could burst.

The excitement was quickly met with the reality of morning sickness—and it wasn't just in the morning. Every evening, like clockwork, I'd barely manage a few bites of dinner before the nausea took over. I'd rush to the bathroom, sick and frustrated, feeling like my body was working against me. This routine dragged on for three long months, making it difficult to enjoy what should've been a glowing time in my life.

I wasn't eating well—sometimes just the smell of food would set me off. But through it all, my mum was my rock. She stepped in with so much love and care, meeting my every need. If I craved something strange or specific, she'd find it without question. If I couldn't stomach a meal, she'd offer alternatives until something sat right. She didn't just feed my body—she nourished my spirit.

Her patience and kindness made all the difference. Looking back, I realize those were some of the most vulnerable moments of my life, and having her there by my side made me feel safe, supported, and deeply loved. Even through the sickness, there was a quiet joy in knowing I was carrying life, and that my daughter, Natasha, was growing stronger each day.

Pregnancy should have been a time of shared joy, of growing together in anticipation of a new life—but for me, it felt like I was walking that path alone. Stuart didn't give me the love and attention I so desperately needed. At a time when I longed for comfort, reassurance, and connection, he withdrew. I didn't understand why he ignored me, why the man I was building a family with hardly spoke a word to me. He never asked how I was feeling, or if I needed anything—not even something as simple as a glass of water.

I was young and unsure, and I didn't know how to bridge the growing silence between us. Stuart was an introvert by nature, but his emotional distance during that time felt like abandonment. While he went off to work, I stayed with Mum during the day—she was my anchor, the only one who seemed to truly see what I was going through. Still, the loneliness crept in.

His absence wasn't just physical—it was emotional, and it hurt deeply. I felt invisible in my own home, in my own relationship. The stress began affecting my health; my blood pressure was all over the place, and the emotional toll started to show. I was carrying so much—physically, emotionally—and I often felt like I was carrying it all alone.

It was a confusing, painful chapter. I needed tenderness, support, a partner who would hold my hand through the uncertainty of first-time motherhood. Instead, I was left to find strength in myself, and in the quiet presence of my mum, who gave all the love I was missing.

Despite the loneliness, despite the silence from Stuart, I wasn't completely alone. It was me—and my baby girl. She was with me the entire time, growing inside me, reminding me with every flutter and every turn that something extraordinary was happening. In the quiet moments, when I felt invisible to the world, I would place my hand on my belly and feel her move, and I knew she could feel me too. That connection gave me strength.

She became the heartbeat I clung to when things felt overwhelming. Her little life gave me purpose when I was drowning in unanswered questions and emotional isolation. I'd whisper to her, telling her how much I loved her already, how I would be there for her, even if I felt like no one was there for me. She was my anchor, my light in the shadows.

Every wave of morning sickness, every lonely night, every tear I shed in silence—it all felt worth it because I had her. She was growing, thriving, and giving me a reason to hold on. My baby girl and I were already a team. In so many ways, she saved me.

Mum stood beside me with unconditional love, but it was my daughter who filled the deepest, quietest spaces in my soul. She was my miracle in the making—my companion through the hardest days, and my reason to believe in brighter ones ahead.

When Natasha was born seven weeks premature, my world stopped. Everything I thought I was prepared for unraveled in an instant. She was so small—so fragile—barely the size of a doll, with translucent skin and tiny fingers curled into fists. I remember the rush of the hospital room, the panic in the nurses' eyes, the quiet urgency in the doctor's voice. I barely had a moment to process it all before they whisked her away to the neonatal intensive care unit.

I didn't get to hold her. That broke me.

I was desperate to touch her, to feel her warmth against my chest, to tell her I was there—but I had to wait. They placed her in an incubator, a clear plastic box filled with wires and tubes that were now keeping my daughter alive. I stood there, staring at her tiny body, feeling helpless and terrified. Her chest rose and fell so fast, like a hummingbird's wings, and I wondered if her little heart could keep up.

Fear consumed me. What if she didn't make it? What if I never got the chance to rock her to sleep, to hear her cry, to kiss her forehead and tell her how deeply I loved her? I blamed myself—wondered if I'd done something wrong, if I could have kept her safe just a little longer.

That night was the longest of my life. I couldn't sleep. I lay in bed, empty arms aching, heart breaking, silently praying over and over again: *Please, let her be okay.*

When I was finally allowed to hold her the next day, tears poured down my cheeks. She was wrapped in wires, still so fragile, but she was mine. And in that moment, feeling her tiny heartbeat against my chest, I made a silent promise: I will fight for you every day of my life.

As the time drew near for Natasha's arrival, my body ached with pain and uncertainty, but I must say—Stuart was there when it mattered most. Despite everything we'd been through, and the emotional distance that lingered between us during my pregnancy, he stood by my side in the delivery room.

I remember the way he held my hand, his fingers trembling slightly, his silence now full of presence rather than absence. He didn't say much—but he didn't leave either. That meant more than words could say. As the contractions surged through me, fear gripped me tightly—especially knowing my baby girl was coming into the world too soon. But having Stuart there, even in quiet support, grounded me in that terrifying moment.

When Natasha was finally born—tiny, vulnerable, and seven weeks early—his eyes welled up with emotion. We both stared at her in awe and fear as she was quickly taken to the incubator. It was a whirlwind, and yet something sacred hung in the air. Despite the struggles in our relationship, in that moment, we were two young parents united by love for the little life we had created.

That memory will always stay with me. It reminded me that even the most complicated people can show up when it counts.

Chapter 5:

Our love blossomed with every shared moment, deepening as we stepped into new chapters together. The arrival of our precious baby girl, Natasha, was a turning point—an overwhelming rush of love that transformed our world. To celebrate this beautiful beginning, we set off on a heartfelt adventure to Australia, eager to mark this new season of life with discovery and joy.

We lived in Cairns initially, soaking in the humidity and heat, adjusting to a new rhythm of life in a new land. Then, with a spirit of exploration, we packed up and left for our travels—to Katherine, Monkey Mia, and beyond.

One of the most unforgettable parts of our time in Katherine was visiting the caves. I still remember the moment we stepped inside—everything just fell silent, except for the occasional drip of water echoing through the chambers. I was completely awe-struck. The walls shimmered under the soft light, and I couldn't stop staring at the limestone formations. They looked like something out of a dream—twisting, towering shapes that had taken thousands of years to form. I had never seen anything like it in my life. And knowing that water—something so gentle—had carved all of it made it even more incredible.

That whole part of our journey felt really supported and safe, thanks to Stuart's family. His parents especially were amazing. They gave us so much love and space, always happy to help with Natasha so we could have a little time to explore just the two of us. It felt like such a gift, especially in a new place. Sometimes, it's the quiet support behind the scenes that makes the adventure possible, you know?

From Katherine, we made our way west to one of the most beautiful places I've ever seen—Shark Bay. That place felt like the edge of the world. The colors were unreal—clear turquoise waters meeting bright white sand, with endless sky above. And it was there that I caught my first shovel-nose shark. I still laugh thinking about how nervous I was. But Stuart was so patient, guiding me through every step, and when I finally felt the tug on the line—I couldn't believe it. It was wild and exciting and completely outside of anything I'd done before. I remember looking over at him, grinning like a kid, and he just smiled back like, "Told you you could do it."

And then there was Monkey Mia—what a name, right? But it was pure magic. We waded into the shallow waters, and before long, these beautiful dolphins swam right up to us. They were so calm, so gentle. Feeding them felt surreal. Natasha couldn't stop giggling—her tiny hands reaching out, eyes wide with wonder. It was one of those moments where everything felt still and perfect, like time had paused just so we could soak it all in.

That chapter of our journey was full of love, discovery, and a deep sense of connection—to nature, to each other, to this new little life we were guiding through the world. From the red dirt of the outback to the sparkling sea, we weren't just seeing Australia—we were living it, together. Hand in hand, we wandered through breathtaking landscapes, uncovered hidden gems, and laughed like children tasting freedom. Every sunset we watched, every road we traveled, felt like a page in our story—etched with happiness, wonder, and love.

After our travels, we lived in Perth for a year, renting a unit. During that time, I worked as a caretaker for a complex of 21 units. For just $50 a month, I handled the maintenance, administration, and helped new tenants settle in. It wasn't much money, but it gave me purpose and kept me engaged with the community. That work, however modest, reminded me of my capability and worth. And it was in Perth that I received my Australian **residency**—a quietly monumental moment. I was no longer just navigating a new country—I was part of it.

Life took another sharp turn when Stuart decided to move us again—this time to the small country town of Cunderdin. The move was abrupt and disorienting, but I had no choice. My life seemed to follow his path, not mine.

Cunderdin became an unexpected turning point for me. It was there that I earned my driver's license—a small but deeply empowering achievement. For the first time, I felt a glimpse of freedom and self-reliance. I also joined the locals for weekend tennis matches, my very first attempt at the sport. I wasn't great at it, but it wasn't about winning. It was about laughter, movement, and carving out something that was just for me.

We spent a few years in a small two-bedroom unit in Cunderdin, Western Australia, trying to start fresh once again. Over time, we began to find our rhythm there. The girls had space to play, I found comfort in the routine, and for a while, it felt like we were finally building something stable. It wasn't perfect, but it was ours.

Then, during our time in Cunderdin, I gave birth to my second daughter—Cassie. She came into the world through a caesarean section, a different experience from Natasha's early and frightening birth. Although it was a surgical delivery, I felt more prepared, more in control, and incredibly grateful for a safe outcome.

But the recovery was brutal. I remember the cold, clinical feel of the operating theatre, the numbness spreading from my spine, and the strange pressure—not pain, but intense tugging and pulling—as they brought my baby girl into the world. The joy of hearing her first cry was real and overwhelming, but what followed was a blur of discomfort and struggle. The surgical pain after the anesthesia wore off was unlike anything I had known. My stomach muscles throbbed with every slight movement. I couldn't sit up without wincing, and walking upright was impossible. I shuffled around, hunched over like an old woman, holding onto furniture for support, doing my best not to cry from the pain.

Simple tasks—standing at the sink, boiling water, even getting out of bed—felt like monumental efforts. I couldn't cook, I could barely care for myself, let alone care for my newborn the way I wanted to. So, I turned to Stuart. I asked him gently, with all the vulnerability in my voice, if he could please make me something to eat. Just something warm, something simple.

He didn't look at me with kindness or concern. Instead, his response was cold and cruel. With a scowl on his face, he slammed a tin of spaghetti on the counter and barked, "HERE. EAT THIS," before storming out of the house. The door echoed behind him like a final slap.

I stood there, barely able to straighten my back, stunned and hurting—not just from the surgery, but from the sting of being treated like I didn't matter. I felt invisible in my own home, dismissed at one of the most vulnerable moments of my life.

But even in that moment of abandonment, I looked down at my tiny baby girl, and I knew I had to keep going. I was in pain, yes, but I had love—deep, fierce love—for the daughter in my arms. And somehow, that love gave me the strength to move forward, even if slowly, even if bent over, step by painful step.

And it was in Cunderdin, four years after arriving in Australia, that I officially became a **citizen**. I still remember the moment the letter arrived from the immigration department. There were no fireworks, no grand parade—but there was something deep and still inside me: a sense of being rooted. Of finally belonging to the soil beneath my feet. I wasn't just a guest anymore. Australia was my home, and I had the paper to prove it.

But when Cassie turned five, everything changed again.

Stuart, my husband, made a sudden decision to uproot our lives and travel from Cunderdin all the way to Toowoomba, Queensland—a journey of 3,962 kilometers. He was chasing a business opportunity with a friend, convinced it would lead to something bigger. It wasn't a decision we made together. Like so many others before it, it was his call, and I had no real say. I packed up our lives once again, leaving behind what little sense of stability we had managed to create.

When we arrived in Toowoomba, we had nowhere permanent to live. I applied for government housing, clinging to the hope of something steady for the girls. The wait felt endless—three long, uncertain months. But when we were finally approved, I couldn't believe what we were given: a rented three-bedroom cottage with polished wooden floors, surrounded by a brown picket fence. It wasn't ours, but it felt like home. For the first time in a long while, I saw more than just shelter—I saw beauty, dignity, and a place where we could finally breathe again.

I opened my heart—and my home—by starting a day care centre from that very house. It became more than just a source of income. It was my way of building something of my own. A place that gave other children care and comfort, and gave us—me and my daughters—a sense of purpose, routine, and quiet strength.

Chapter 6:

As time passed, something began to shift—quietly at first, then unmistakably. Stuart grew more distant, his attention consumed by the business venture he had thrown himself into. What hurt the most wasn't just his distraction—it was the silence that came with it. The lack of communication. The secrets. The way plans were made and futures were drawn up, and somehow, I wasn't part of the picture.

I felt it every day—in the way he no longer looked up when I spoke, in the way the kids' laughter no longer pulled him into the moment like it used to. It was like watching someone you love drift slowly out to sea, and no matter how loud you screamed from the shore, they just kept paddling away.

Resentment took root in my heart. Anger followed. Not just because I felt abandoned as a partner, but because I saw the gap widening between him and our children. Their innocent need for his time and affection went unnoticed, and I felt powerless to shield them from the ache of that absence.

I carried that hurt alone, burying it under the demands of motherhood and survival. But the weight of his neglect—of being emotionally sidelined in a life we were supposed to be building together—was heavy, and it left deep cracks in the foundation of our family.

Through it all—the silence, the distance, the aching loneliness—I never let go of the one thing that mattered most: being a mother. I poured every ounce of love I had into my daughters. When the world felt uncertain and unstable, I made sure they had a place where they always felt safe, heard, and unconditionally loved. I was their steady ground, their refuge, their home.

There were nights I cried silently after they went to bed, my heart breaking under the weight of everything I had to carry alone. But the next morning, I would rise, smile, and braid their hair like nothing was wrong—because their peace was more important than my pain.

Their laughter became my medicine. Their hugs, my sanctuary. Every giggle, every bedtime story, every whispered "I love you, Mum" stitched my heart back together, one thread at a time. They reminded me that I mattered, even when I felt invisible to the one person who once promised forever.

Despite the storm around us, I was unwavering. I showed up every single day—with love, with compassion, and with the quiet power of a woman who refuses to let her children feel unloved, unseen, or unimportant. My strength wasn't loud—it was found in soft hands, patient words, and the fierce fire of a mother's devotion. And in their smiles, I found proof that I was doing something right.

He was there physically, but emotionally, it felt like he had vanished. His presence brought no comfort—only a growing void that deepened with each passing day. I felt like a single mother inside my own marriage. The emotional distance was suffocating. There's a unique kind of pain in loving someone who's drifting further away, even as you sit next to them on the same couch.

In that space, I reclaimed a part of myself. I transformed our home into a place not just of safety, but of purpose. Driven by my love for children and my longing for both flexibility and stability, I decided to open a home daycare. I enrolled in a Certificate III in Early Childhood Education and Care. Every lesson I studied—about development, safety, emotional well-being—felt personal, because I was living it, both as a mother and a woman finding her way.

But beneath the accomplishments, there was still a quiet ache. It's hard to explain the heartbreak of feeling emotionally alone while still sharing a life with someone. I did everything I could to keep us afloat, to hold the family together—but sometimes I wondered if anyone saw just how hard I was trying. The emotional weight was immense, but I carried it—because my daughters needed me, and I refused to let them feel the same emptiness I was drowning in.

I carried a weight most people never saw.

While he chased dreams abroad—flying to the States with his business partner, disappearing for weeks at a time—I was left to hold everything together. The house. The children. The bills. The invisible labor that builds a life.

So I sought comfort in my day care centre. What started as a way to make ends meet turned into something much more. I created a day care—not in a shiny building with bright signs or expensive toys, but in a home filled with warmth, quiet strength, and stories of survival. It was never just about supervision. I was creating a space that felt safe, not just for the children who walked through the door, but for myself too. I wasn't just watching over little ones—I was building a life. One that was mine.

Not just because I needed the income, but because I've always had a nurturing soul. Children brought light into the house, even on days when my own heart felt dim. Their giggles echoed through the rooms like music, their curiosity pulled me out of my own tired thoughts. They made the space feel alive again. Their needs gave me focus. Their presence gave me hope.

And I wanted to do it right. If I was going to care for them, I had to give them the best of me. So I threw myself into learning. I enrolled in a Certificate III in Early Childhood Education and Care. Every module, every assignment, was a step back toward myself. It wasn't just a qualification—it was a lifeline. I studied child development, emotional wellness, health, safety, inclusion. I learned how to build community and offer care not just with structure, but with genuine love.

Those lessons weren't just for the children. They became soft reminders to care for myself—to tend to the emotional wounds I so often ignored. To remember that I mattered too, even if no one else said it out loud.

But it was isolating. Achingly so. I felt like a single mother in a marriage that no longer felt like a partnership. The emotional loneliness ran deeper than silence—it was the absence of connection. He rarely spoke of his business, his finances, or his thoughts. The secrecy carved out a chasm between us, and every trip to the States felt like him leaving a little more of us behind.

Still, I pressed on.

My days were filled with nap schedules, nappy changes, lesson plans, and paperwork. I juggled the needs of other parents, other children, and my own precious girls—who were growing up watching their mum give all of herself, every single day.

Evenings were my escape. Twice a week, I'd lace up my shoes and head to the local hall to play badminton. Just a couple of hours, but it felt like breathing again. The rhythm of the game, the sound of the shuttlecock slicing the air, the laughs shared with strangers who slowly became familiar faces—those moments grounded me. My girls came with me, watching from the sidelines, making friends of their own. It wasn't just exercise; it was therapy. It was release.

I invited him, hoping to bridge the distance. To reconnect. But he always declined. He remained apart, emotionally distant, like a ghost passing through the life we once built together. He came back from his trips not with stories or excitement—but with silence, as though home had become a place of obligation, not joy.

And yet, despite the loneliness, despite the burdens, I was proud. Proud of what I had built. Proud of how I kept going. Proud of the kind of mother I was. I was not just surviving—I was quietly thriving in the spaces I had carved out for myself.

Because sometimes, strength isn't loud. Sometimes it's the woman who carries the world on her back, smiles at her children, and still finds time to chase a shuttle across a court—just to feel alive.

After everything we'd been through, I wanted to believe that love could still survive. I held onto hope—not for fairy tales, but for healing. For honesty. For something real.

Chapter 7:

The vibrant energy that once flowed so freely between us began to dim. He grew more distant, his thoughts seemingly elsewhere. The man who once held my hand tightly now seemed distracted, and the emotional rhythm we once moved to together felt slightly offbeat. I began to feel like a spectator in his world, no longer at the center of it.

We didn't sleep together anymore. He had moved onto the lounge, and that quiet shift—his body no longer beside mine at night—spoke louder than any argument could have. The bed felt colder, the silence heavier. We lived in the same house, but it felt like we were worlds apart.

Still, I cooked his meals. I washed his clothes. I kept the household moving as if we were still a team, even though the connection between us had unraveled. There was no shouting, no explosive fights—just an aching silence. The kind that creeps in slowly and settles deep, until it becomes the background noise of your life.

I kept hoping for a conversation, a breakthrough, *something* to bring us back to each other. But days turned into weeks, and still—we barely spoke. I was living with a man I once loved deeply, who now felt like a stranger passing through my home.

I felt our bond slowly unravel. There were no harsh words, no dramatic moments—just a growing silence, an ache I couldn't name but could feel in my bones. The harmony that once defined us was slipping through my fingers, and no matter how tightly I tried to hold on, I could sense I was losing him, little by little.

For fourteen years, we built a life together. Stuart was not just my husband—he was my partner, my confidant, the person I believed I could rely on through anything. Together, we had weathered life's storms and celebrated its joys. I truly thought we were in it for the long haul.

Just as I had begun to feel a sense of peace—like maybe, finally, I had found my safe haven—life delivered another unexpected and devastating blow. Stuart told me he wanted to move to the United States with a friend to start a new business. At first, I tried to be supportive, believing it was a temporary opportunity, a new chapter that we would navigate as a couple.

But the truth cut much deeper. This wasn't about business. It wasn't about ambition. It was about someone else. He had met another woman—an American—and he intended to marry her.

The devastation I felt was unlike anything I had ever known—deep, hollow, and all-consuming. It was the kind of heartbreak that doesn't just break your heart; it crushes your spirit. It seeps into your bones, into your breath, until even the act of existing becomes unbearable.

I remember standing in our kitchen, that quiet little corner of our home where we had once shared late-night cups of tea and whispered dreams. But now, the silence between us was suffocating. The very air felt heavy, as though the walls themselves were mourning with me. I could feel the distance between us like a canyon I hadn't noticed growing. And now, I was staring across it, reaching for someone who no longer wanted to be held.

My voice shook as I tried to hold myself together, tried to hold *us* together.

"What have I done wrong, Stuart?" I whispered, my throat tight, the question carrying the weight of my shattered heart. "Tell me. Was I not enough? Was I too much? Just… tell me what I did."

I watched him closely, praying for a flicker of regret in his eyes, something—*anything*—that would show he was still mine, even if just a little. But there was none. His face was calm, almost blank, like he had already grieved me and moved on.

"You didn't do anything wrong," he said softly, eyes avoiding mine like they carried a truth too cruel to meet. "You've been good to me… You were a good wife. A good mother."

That single word echoed inside me like a scream. I felt something collapse in my chest. I was no longer his present. No longer his future. Just a past he was gently trying to step away from.

"Then why are you leaving me?" I asked, my voice cracking, my breath short as if each word scraped its way out of me. "Why her? Why now?"

He sighed deeply, and for a second, I thought I saw pain in his expression—but it wasn't the kind that brought him back. It was the kind people wear when they've made peace with breaking someone else.

"I don't know how to explain it," he said. "My feelings… they changed. I didn't plan this. It just happened."

Each word was like a cold slap. Love that "just happens" can also "just disappear"—and I was the casualty of that fading spark.

I stepped toward him, desperation clinging to my every move, my every word.

"We've built a life together. Fourteen years, Stuart. Doesn't that mean anything to you?"

I searched his face for something to hold onto—a twitch of guilt, a flicker of love. But all I saw was pity. And that was worse than hate.

"Please," he said, his voice quiet, almost pleading. "If you love me… set me free."

It felt as if time stopped.

Set you free?

The man I had loved, supported, and trusted was standing in front of me, not asking for forgiveness or another chance, but for release—as if our marriage had been a cage, as if *I* had been the one holding him back.

"Set you free?" I repeated, my voice hollow, stunned. "Is that what love means to you now—letting you walk out on everything we promised, everything we built together?"

No reply. Only silence. A silence so thick it felt like grief.

And I knew. Deep down, I knew I could not make someone stay who no longer wanted to be kept. You can't beg for love that has left the room.

We got divorced.

Just like that, the life I had clung to unraveled at the seams. The man I once called my soulmate, my partner in every dream and struggle, packed up his world and moved to the United States—to start anew with someone else. An American blonde woman who would become his new beginning while I was left to mourn what had become my ending.

I stood amidst the remnants of what once was—a wedding ring tucked in a drawer, photos too painful to look at, rooms that echoed with absence—and I realized I was alone again. Not just without him, but without the version of myself that had believed love would finally stay.

Chapter 8:

After the divorce, Stuart didn't pay any child support for
Natasha and Cassie. Not a single cent.
It was as if, in walking away from me, he had also walked
away from them—from his own daughters.

One evening, after yet another overdue bill and a tearful
conversation with the school about unpaid fees, I finally
confronted him. He was sitting in the lounge, scrolling on
his phone, as though the world wasn't burning quietly
around me.

"Stuart," I said, trying to keep my voice calm, "we need to
talk about child support. The girls need things. School
uniforms, lunches, shoes—they're growing. They need
you."

He looked up slowly, barely meeting my eyes. "I don't
have much right now. Things are tight with the business."

I stared at him, stunned. "You're flying back and forth
between countries and setting up a business, but you can't
help with your own children?"

He sighed, as if I was burdening him. "I'm doing what I
can. I'm not making a salary yet. Besides… you always
managed, didn't you?"

That hit me like a slap. "Yes, I managed," I said, my voice
rising now. "I managed while you were gone, chasing your
dreams. I held this family together, Stuart. You think this
house ran on magic? That food just appeared on the table? I
gave everything so you could build your empire—and now
you've built it without us."

He looked away, jaw tight. "I didn't want to talk about this."

"Of course you didn't," I snapped. "Because you never told me anything about your income. You were too scared I'd claim something. But I didn't even know I could. I didn't know my rights. I didn't have anyone to tell me. I was just trying to survive."

And then he looked me dead in the eye, with a sharpness I hadn't seen before.
"You come from nothing," he said coldly. "So, you deserve nothing."

I felt the words slice through me—quiet, venomous, final. I stared at him, heart pounding, unable to speak for a moment.

"You really believe that?" I whispered, shaking. "That I don't deserve anything? After everything I gave up for you? For this family?"

He didn't say a word. Just stared at the floor like a child being scolded. No apology. No acknowledgment. Just silence.

And then came the part that still burns, even now.
The night he came back—not with flowers or remorse—but with a duffel bag in his hand and no place else to go.

He stood at my doorstep, eyes tired, voice low. "Can I stay for a few days? Just until I figure something out?"

I should've slammed the door. But I didn't. I stood there, trembling, torn between rage and the familiar ache of hope.

"Why here, Stuart?" I asked, blinking back the tears. "Why come back to the woman you left?"

"Because I didn't know where else to go," he said simply, his voice hollow.

That was all I was in the end—a safety net. A shelter. "You're not here for me. Or for the girls. You're here because you've run out of options."

He didn't argue.

I stepped aside, and he walked in—into the house he had left behind, into the life he abandoned—like a guest. No apology. No explanation. Just a man looking for somewhere to sleep.

I wasn't stupid. I was loyal. I was hopeful. I was holding onto the belief that someone I once shared a life with would at least be fair. And when he wasn't, I learned—again— that some lessons come the hard way.

It didn't break me. But it did change me. It made me sharper. Wiser. Less willing to shrink myself for the sake of someone else's comfort.

Then the news came, they had welcomed a baby girl. Seeing pictures of them together—smiling, glowing, wrapped in the warmth of a new beginning—felt like a knife twisting slowly in my chest. They looked like a complete family, whole and happy, living the very life I had once dreamed of and fought to preserve. I would stare at those pictures longer than I should have, tears stinging my eyes, wondering how easily I had been replaced. It wasn't just the betrayal—it was the ease with which he seemed to move on, as though our years together were just a chapter he could close without looking back.

But while my heart ached, I knew I couldn't allow myself to be swallowed by the pain. I had two daughters who needed me, who looked up to me, whose eyes searched mine every day for reassurance, for love, for strength. And so, I stood back up. I had no choice.

I poured myself into my work as a daycare mum, giving every ounce of my energy to the children in my care and even more to the two who called me Mum. My daughters became my lifeline, the very reason I kept going. Their laughter, their innocence, their unwavering love pulled me back from the edge time and time again. I may have been broken, but I was not defeated—not as long as they needed me.

The days were long and grueling. I was constantly exhausted, not just from the physical demands of work, but from the emotional weight I carried each day. There were nights I lay awake, calculating bills in my head, worrying about rent, about food, about the cost of their school uniforms. Financial stress loomed over me like a shadow. Utility bills stacked up. Groceries felt like a luxury. But I made a silent vow to myself: my daughters would not suffer. They would receive a good education. They would feel safe. They would know—always—that they were deeply, unconditionally loved.

The betrayal cut deeper than I could ever have imagined. It wasn't just a broken marriage—it was the breaking of promises, the shattering of dreams we had once whispered into each other's ears. It was the casual way he walked away from the life we had built together, leaving me to pick up the pieces alone. He told me I had done nothing wrong.

In his eyes, I had been a good wife, a good mother. But his love, he said, had faded. And then came the final blow: if I loved him, I'd let him go.

It felt like a cruel irony—being asked to prove my love by allowing him to leave. I felt discarded, as though our years together—our family, our sacrifices, our joys—meant nothing in the face of his newfound happiness. The silence he left behind echoed louder than any words he could have spoken.

But still, I rose. I learned to survive the ache, to live through the storm, and slowly—one step at a time—I began to rediscover my own strength.

The pain didn't just fade—it lingered, settling deep inside like an ache I carried around each day. There were mornings I'd wake up and forget, just for a moment. I'd roll over expecting to hear him breathing beside me, to feel the weight of our old life. But the silence was deafening, and reality would come crashing back in.

Still, I didn't have the luxury of breaking down. I had two daughters who needed me—who looked up at me with wide, trusting eyes that deserved more than my sadness. So, I held it together for them. I made breakfast, packed lunches, kissed their cheeks, and held their tiny hands while quietly holding together the pieces of my own heart.

I threw myself into work—not just to pay the bills, but because I had to keep going. I had to feel useful, to stay busy, to silence the thoughts that crept in when everything went still. But even in the middle of the noise and the routine, I'd sometimes catch myself remembering—us laughing in the kitchen, or dancing in the living room while the girls clapped along. Those memories hit hard. They were sweet but sharp, like holding something beautiful that also stung.

And yet, I was grateful for them. Because they were real. They mattered. Even if he chose to walk away, what we shared had been true once. I held onto that for a while—until it didn't hurt so much.

There were nights I cried myself to sleep after the girls had drifted off, hugging their teddy bears, completely unaware of how broken I felt. And every time I wanted to give up, I reminded myself: I'm their only constant now. They didn't ask for this. They didn't deserve the confusion, the missing pieces, the quiet sadness that sometimes settled over our home like fog.

So, I smiled through the pain. I laughed when they laughed. I held them a little tighter when they needed comfort—and even tighter when I did. I promised myself that I'd make sure they never felt unloved or abandoned. If they asked why their dad was gone, I'd find gentle ways to explain it without letting bitterness spill into their hearts.

And slowly, something shifted. Somewhere deep within, I started to feel the tiniest flicker of strength. Not confidence exactly—but something close. Maybe it was hope. Maybe just the instinct to protect and survive. I didn't know who I was without the marriage, without the life we'd planned. But I was learning, step by step.

What I did know was this: my daughters were my reason. Their giggles, their soft sleepy voices calling out "Mama," their belief in me even when I felt like I had nothing left to give—that's what kept me moving forward. I didn't need to be perfect. I just needed to be present. And that, I could do.

Part 2

Marriage: Round Two

Chapter 9:

At first, I didn't know how to move on. I was simply surviving—getting through one day at a time, pretending I had it all under control when inside, I often felt lost. The future was this wide, empty space, and I didn't know how to fill it. But something remarkable happened in those quiet, broken moments: I began to hear my own voice again.

It didn't come all at once. It came in whispers.

It came when I looked in the mirror one morning and didn't see someone abandoned—I saw someone still standing.

It came in the calm after I tucked my daughters into bed, and I sat alone with a cup of tea, exhausted but proud that I'd made it through another day.

It came when I realized that moving on didn't mean forgetting, or pretending none of it happened. It meant reclaiming the parts of myself I'd given away, piece by piece, over the years. It meant learning to love the woman I was becoming—stronger, wiser, softer in some ways, but fiercer in others.

Courage didn't show up like a lightning bolt. It showed up in small, quiet choices. Choosing to wake up and keep going. Choosing to smile when I didn't feel like it, not to hide the pain, but to remind myself that joy still had a place in my life. Choosing to speak kindly to myself when the world felt harsh. Choosing to believe—however uncertainly—that there was still more waiting for me.

I started doing little things for myself. I took walks. I wrote down my feelings. I reconnected with old friends, the kind who reminded me of who I was before life broke me open. I let myself dream again, cautiously at first, then with growing confidence. I didn't know exactly where I was heading, but I knew I didn't want to stay stuck in the past.

Moving on wasn't about being fearless. It was about being brave *despite* the fear. It was about saying, "This hurt me—but it didn't destroy me." It was about giving myself permission to hope again, to trust that healing wasn't just possible, it was already happening—quietly, patiently, one heartbeat at a time.

And somewhere along the way, I stopped surviving and started living again.

One day, a chance encounter quietly shifted the course of my life. I was on a bus, heading to visit my sister, my thoughts tangled in worry and weariness. I had become used to the silence around me, lost in my own world. Then, a soft voice broke through the hum of the engine. "May I sit next to you?" the man asked.

It was such a simple question, the kind that usually comes and goes without much thought—but there was something about the way he asked it. His tone was gentle, respectful, almost careful, as if he could sense the walls, I had built around myself. I looked up, surprised by the kindness in his eyes, and nodded. "Yes," I replied.

At the time, I had no idea that this quiet moment, this one word, would mark the beginning of something entirely new.

Kurt and I started with small talk—safe, polite conversation between strangers—but somehow, it felt different. His presence was calm, comforting. There was no pressure, no expectation. Just two people sharing a space and a few kind words. Before I stepped off the bus, we exchanged numbers. I wasn't sure why I said yes. Maybe it was curiosity, maybe it was hope. But I'm grateful I did.

In the days that followed, we began talking regularly. What started as casual conversations slowly turned into something deeper. He made me laugh—really laugh, the kind that felt like a breath of fresh air after being underwater for too long. I began looking forward to his calls. His voice brought a sense of calm that settled the ache in my chest.

There was no grand declaration, no sweeping gestures. Just patience, warmth, and the steady unfolding of trust. He didn't ask me to forget the past or pretend I hadn't been hurt. Instead, he gave me space to be exactly where I was. For the first time in a long time, I felt heard, seen—not as someone broken, but as someone worthy of gentle love.

I had been so focused on surviving, on holding everything together for my daughters, that I had forgotten what it felt like to be noticed just for being me. Not as a mother, not as a worker, not as someone who had been left behind—but as a woman with stories, dreams, and a heart still capable of beating.

Meeting him didn't erase the pain, but it reminded me that healing was possible. That joy could return, slowly and unexpectedly. And that sometimes, all it takes is a single moment—one quiet question, one soft smile, one word: "Yes."

One day, while we were sitting on a park bench, watching the last golden light of the afternoon filter through the trees, he turned to me with a quiet seriousness in his eyes. For a moment, he just looked at me, as though searching for the right words.

Then, softly, Kurt asked, "Do you want to be a family again?"

I froze. My heart skipped a beat.

I stared at him, my breath caught somewhere between my chest and throat. "What... what do you mean?" I whispered, afraid to hope, afraid I had misunderstood.

He reached for my hand, holding it gently in his. "I mean... with me. Us. To share a life—not just conversations or dinners or holidays. A home. A future. I want to grow old with you, to be there through everything. Not as someone passing through your life, but staying. Really staying."

My eyes welled with tears. His voice was so calm, so certain, but I could see the vulnerability beneath it. He wasn't just asking for love—he was offering it, fully and without conditions.

The weight of everything I had carried—the years of abandonment, the betrayal, the loneliness—all seemed to press on me at once. My mind swirled with doubt: *Could I trust again? Could I let someone in, after all the pain?*

But in my heart, something had already begun to soften.

I nodded slowly, then whispered, "Yes... I want that too."

"You do?" he asked, a breath of relief escaping him as he smiled, eyes brimming with emotion.

"I do," I said again, more certain this time. "I want peace. I want love that doesn't walk away when things get hard. I want to build something real—with someone who truly sees me."

That decision led us to a quiet, intimate backyard wedding, surrounded by close friends and family. We chose a small patch of land near the coast—pristine beaches on one side, tall green trees on the other. The ceremony was simple, but perfect. The sky turned a soft lavender as we exchanged our vows.

As I stood there, my hands in his, I looked at the man before me—the one who had patiently waited, who had never rushed my healing—and I felt a deep, still joy. The breeze kissed our cheeks, the waves hummed in the distance, and for the first time in a long time, I felt held. Not just by him, but by life itself.

"I promise to never give up on us," he said, his voice trembling.

"And I promise to trust again," I replied, tears falling freely. "To believe in love, because you taught me it still exists."

The view around us was breathtaking—but it was the love in that moment that made it feel like paradise.

Chapter 10:

Our life began with a kind of beauty I had only ever dreamed of. We spent countless evenings strolling hand-in-hand along the shoreline, the waves lapping at our feet as the sun dipped below the horizon, painting the sky in shades of amber and rose. Those moments—simple, quiet, full of peace—wrapped around my heart like a warm blanket. For the first time in years, I wasn't surviving; I was truly living. I felt whole again. Safe. Loved.

After meeting Kurt, I made the bittersweet decision to close my daycare center. It had served its purpose—it helped me stand on my own feet when I needed it most—but it was time to step into a new chapter. I packed up our life, left Toowoomba behind, and moved to Noosa. There, amidst the ocean breeze and tropical sunlight, Kurt and I got married.

Kurt believed in me in ways no one ever had before. When he bought a women's boutique shop in Noosa, he looked at me with a soft smile and said, *"I want us to build something together."* That one sentence lit a fire in me. He wasn't just offering me a role in a business—he was offering me trust, partnership, and a future we could shape side by side.

I poured my heart into that boutique. Every dress, every conversation with a customer, every little detail mattered. I learned how to arrange displays that drew people in, how to listen closely to what a woman needed—not just in fashion, but in how she wanted to feel. I began to notice how eyes lit up when someone slipped into a dress that fit just right, when they stood a little taller, smiled a little wider. I was helping people feel seen and beautiful—and, in turn, I began to feel that way myself.

For the first time in a long time, I felt proud of who I was becoming. I wasn't just someone rebuilding her life—I was a woman stepping into her strength. I started walking differently, speaking more confidently. I no longer introduced myself with a shadow of my past hanging over me. I was a mother, yes. But also, a businesswoman. A creator. A woman worthy of love and success.

The boutique became more than just a shop. It was my sanctuary, my proof that healing was possible. That reinvention wasn't just for stories—it could be real, and it could be mine.

My daughters adapted to the move with a resilience that both surprised and inspired me. Starting high school in Noosa wasn't easy—new faces, new routines—but they found their footing quickly. I watched them form friendships, join clubs, and slowly make this coastal town their own. There was something healing in seeing them laugh more freely, walk with confidence, and come home with stories about their day. It reminded me that this fresh start wasn't just mine—it was ours.

Looking back, I can see how life had tested me in every imaginable way—pushing me to the edge, daring me to break. And yet, each hardship came with a hidden gift: a lesson, a tool, a piece of strength I didn't know I possessed. The pain of my past wasn't erased, but it no longer ruled me. Instead, it had become part of the mosaic of who I was—a testament to my endurance, a quiet but constant reminder of how far I had come. In this new chapter, I was no longer just surviving—I was living with purpose, wiser and more grounded than ever before.

But as life would have it, just when peace seemed to settle in, reality knocked on the door again.

After three months of pouring my heart into the apparel business, the truth became hard to ignore. The shop wasn't bringing in enough to sustain us—not enough for rent, for groceries, for the endless stream of bills. Every day was a blur of 12-hour shifts, folding clothes, smiling through the fatigue, hoping the next customer might be the one who turned it all around. But deep inside, I knew we were slipping.

When the boutique couldn't keep us afloat, I did what I had always done—I adapted.

Kurt and I started a commercial laundry business, washing towels, linens, and sheets for hotels and motels. It was far from glamorous, but it was necessary. Clean laundry didn't require a storefront window or perfect lighting. It just needed commitment—and I had plenty of that.

The work was brutal. There were no set hours, just an endless cycle of wash, dry, fold, repeat. I was on my feet for sixteen hours a day, seven days a week. My hands grew raw from the constant contact with detergent and bleach. The scent of industrial soap embedded itself into my skin. There was no makeup, no polished image—just sweat, steam, and survival.

The machines roared like restless beasts, never silent, never still. Large loads of stained towels would come in early morning and leave by nightfall, neatly folded and sealed in plastic. I took pride in that small transformation—filth into freshness. It reminded me of my own story, in a way. Worn down, yes, but not ruined. Not beyond saving.

I barely ate. I barely slept. Every time I closed my eyes, I saw more laundry—never-ending piles waiting to be sorted, cleaned, folded. But I kept going, because stopping wasn't an option. Bills didn't wait. Hunger didn't wait. And I had made a promise to myself: I would never go back to depending on anyone else to save me.

This business wasn't a dream, but it was a lifeline. It taught me that dignity doesn't come from the type of work you do, but from how you do it. I worked with purpose, even when no one was watching. Especially then.

Some people thought I was crazy, working like that. But they didn't understand. I wasn't just building a business—I was building a future I could believe in. Something real. Something mine.

Stress weighed heavily on me, pressing down until I could barely breathe. My body began to show the strain— headaches that pulsed behind my eyes, blood pressure that spiked and dipped unpredictably, nights where sleep refused to come. I was mentally and physically exhausted, and the uncertainty of our future loomed like a shadow I couldn't shake.

And yet, in the middle of that struggle, something beautiful sustained me—my daughters.

Watching them grow into thoughtful, brilliant young women gave me a reason to keep going. I found strength in their strength. I helped with homework and school projects, showed up at every parent-teacher meeting, clapped the loudest at their award ceremonies. I became their biggest cheerleader and quiet guide. The joy on their faces after a good grade or a successful presentation breathed life into me on the days, I felt empty.

Our bond deepened with each passing challenge. We talked late into the nights, shared stories, fears, and dreams. They confided in me, and I found healing in their trust. Despite everything that had fallen apart in my life, this—my relationship with them—was the one thing that had only grown stronger. Their success lit a fire in me. It reminded me that love, support, and unwavering presence could be the greatest foundation of all.

They gave me purpose. They gave me hope. And in many ways, they were the light that led me out of the dark.

One day, after yet another grueling twelve-hour shift, I found myself at my breaking point. My body ached in places I didn't even know could ache. My mind felt like it was unraveling—thread by thread. I was drained, both physically and emotionally, and the weight of everything I was carrying—our business, our home, our future—was pressing down on me like a boulder.

That evening, I sat down with Kurt, hands trembling, heart heavy. My voice was soft but cracked under the weight of desperation.

"Kurt," I began cautiously, "I need to talk to you about something important."

He looked up from his phone, brows raised. "What's going on?"

I hesitated, gathering the last of my courage. "I've been working 12 hours a day, six days a week… I'm exhausted, Kurt. I don't even have time to breathe. I need something to hold onto—some form of wage, like the others get. Just something… to feel seen. To feel valued."

For a moment, there was silence between us, thick and suffocating.

He sighed; his tone clipped. "If I start paying you a wage, we won't be able to save for a house. You know that."

His words hit me like a cold slap.

"So, my wellbeing… my health… it doesn't matter?" I asked, my voice cracking as tears welled up in my eyes. "I'm not asking for luxuries, Kurt. I'm asking for some dignity."

"Your part of this family," he replied, almost dismissively. "Why should I pay you like an outsider when everything we're building is for both of us?"

"But I'm drowning," I whispered, tears now spilling freely. "Every day, I push myself beyond my limits. I give this business everything, and yet, I feel invisible. Do you even see how hard this is for me?"

He looked away, unable—or unwilling—to meet my gaze. That silence cut deeper than any words ever could.

In that moment, something shifted in me. I felt hollow, like all the fight had drained from my body. I wasn't just tired—I was unheard, unseen, and undervalued. The very foundation of our partnership felt like it had cracked beneath me. I had poured myself into this life, hoping it would give me a sense of belonging, of shared purpose. But now, all I felt was isolation.

I began to long—not for luxury or ease—but for recognition, for freedom, for the right to reclaim myself. The woman I had once been—the fighter, the dreamer, the survivor—was still there. And she was starting to whisper again, reminding me that I deserved more than exhaustion in exchange for silence.

Chapter 11:

After endless days and nights pouring my soul into the laundry—scrubbing, folding, organizing, managing—I never imagined I'd be blindsided like that. I was wiping down the front counter, lost in routine, when a well-dressed couple walked in, looking around with curiosity, whispering to each other as they examined the machines and peeked into the back room.

"Can I help you?" I asked, confused.

The woman smiled politely. "We're here to look at the place—it's listed for sale, right?"

I froze. "Excuse me?"

My heart thundered in my chest. I walked outside, scanned the street, and there he was—Kurt, casually leaning against his car like it was just another day. Rage welled up inside me like a tidal wave.

I stormed up to him. "You bastard," I hissed. "You're selling the laundry? Secretly? After everything I've put into this place?"

He looked caught off guard, but not enough. His face was unreadable, cold.

I shook my head, voice cracking. "I've had enough, Kurt. I'm done."

Without another word, I walked away—out of the laundry, out of the life we had tried to build, out of the illusion I had clung to for too long.

We separated that day. And two years later, I filed for divorce. It wasn't just the end of our marriage—it was the beginning of reclaiming myself.

Our relationship was already strained—fragile, filled with silences that spoke louder than words. This was the final blow. I could no longer ignore the signs, no longer sacrifice myself in the hope that things might return to the way they were. I was emotionally exhausted, mentally drained, and desperate for air—real air, the kind that fills your lungs and reminds you you're alive, not just surviving.

Later, Kurt told me the couple who bought the laundry went broke—so, conveniently, I wouldn't be getting my share. But deep down, I knew he was lying. Still, I didn't have the strength to fight it then. I was in the hospital, my head cut open, half of my hair shaved, a surgeon having gone into my brain to stop the bleeding and placed a coil clip to save my life. Money was the last thing on my mind—I was just trying to survive.

One afternoon, as I lay in that hospital bed, dazed and fragile, Kurt showed up. He stood by the door with that same rehearsed sorrow in his eyes.

"Please," he whispered, "just come back to me. We can fix this."

I turned my face toward the wall, fury bubbling just beneath the surface. I slowly looked at him and said, coldly, "Get out. Get out of here now—or I'll call the nurses."

He hesitated, like he didn't believe me.

"I mean it, Kurt," I said, louder this time. "Leave. You've done enough."

He walked out, and I never looked back. Even in my most broken physical state, I knew: going back would have broken my spirit beyond repair.

Two years of distance gave me the space I desperately needed—to heal, to reflect, to reclaim the pieces of myself I had lost. I poured myself into self-care, into reconnecting with my daughters, into learning what peace really feels like when you stop fighting battles that aren't yours to fight.

Walking away from that commercial laundry wasn't just leaving a job or a business—it was leaving behind a version of myself who had endured enough. And in her place, I began to rebuild someone stronger, someone softer in all the right places, and fiercer where it mattered most.

The separation marked more than just the end of a marriage—it marked the beginning of a new chapter for me and my daughters. It was not easy. Every day brought its own set of challenges—uncertainties about money, moments of self-doubt, and the quiet ache of starting over. But with each sunrise, I found myself growing stronger.

I learned how to manage my finances on my own, step by step—paying the bills, budgeting groceries, making sure my daughters had everything they needed. It wasn't perfect, but it was mine. And that gave me a sense of pride I hadn't felt in years.

I found a new job—one that didn't drain me, one that gave me structure, purpose, and the dignity I had been longing for. The routine, the people, the independence—it all slowly helped me rebuild my self-confidence. I began to recognize myself again—not just as a mother, not just as someone's wife, but as a woman with her own strength, voice, and dreams.

And during this healing, a painful truth settled into my heart: he hadn't married me for love. He had married me as a worker. Someone to hold up his world, to carry the weight of his dreams on my back without ever being acknowledged for it. I had mistaken shared effort for shared life. But looking back, it was clear—my value to him was measured in hours worked, not in the love or partnership I had so freely given. It hurt, deeply. But that realization also set me free.

Because from that moment on, I stopped blaming myself. I stopped wondering what more I could have done. I had given everything I had—my time, my energy, my care— and still, it hadn't been enough for someone who never truly saw me. And so, I started choosing me.

Chapter 12:

Determined to seek justice, I finally gathered the courage to seek legal advice. It wasn't an easy decision. I wrestled with guilt, fear, and that lingering hope that maybe things could still be salvaged. But the truth was clearer than ever: I had been taken for granted. My sacrifices, my endless hours of work, my silence in the face of disrespect—they had been mistaken for weakness.

When my husband received the letter from the solicitor, his reaction was swift and shocking—he attempted to take his own life. For a moment, I was paralyzed by fear and confusion. But deep down, I recognized it for what it was: emotional blackmail, an act of manipulation intended to regain control over me. It wasn't love—it was power.

I stood at a crossroads, knowing that if I turned back, I would lose myself again. And so, I chose to move forward. I filed for divorce.

The process was grueling. I was filled with emotional turmoil—waves of sadness, betrayal, anger, and disappointment. I had poured myself into the marriage, into the business, into building a life together. But in the end, I was left feeling undervalued and invisible.

Despite the countless hours I had worked, the responsibilities I had shouldered, and the personal sacrifices I had made, I was never treated as an equal—not in the relationship, and certainly not in the business. I wasn't listed as an owner. My efforts, though essential, were seen as secondary. My voice was never truly heard.

Filing for divorce wasn't just an end—it was a declaration. A moment where I reclaimed my worth. I wasn't just walking away from a man—I was walking away from the belief that I had to settle for less. I had stayed too long in a place that didn't value my heart, my labor, or my humanity.

Visiting him in the hospital was one of the most difficult and emotionally conflicting experiences of my life. I walked in carrying a heavy heart—one filled with sadness, guilt, confusion, and deep fatigue. I reminded myself that I was not responsible for his choices. His pain, while tragic, did not erase mine. My safety—both emotional and physical—had to come first.

After two long years of separation, I found the strength to finally file for divorce. It was not a decision I made lightly. The journey there had been paved with sleepless nights, moments of self-doubt, and waves of heartbreak. But filing for divorce became something more than a legal process— it was an act of self-respect. It was me choosing to no longer shrink myself for the comfort of others. It was me saying, "I matter too."

Though the divorce marked the end of a painful chapter, it was also the beginning of something new. A breath of fresh air after years of suffocating silence. It allowed me to finally prioritize myself and my daughters, free from the emotional chaos of a toxic and unequal relationship. For the first time in a long time, I could breathe, I could think clearly, and I could dream again.

It wasn't just about leaving a marriage—it was about returning to myself.

I began to understand that divorce wasn't a sign of failure; it was a courageous step toward healing. It was a declaration that I deserved peace, joy, and a life that honored my worth. And in that moment of clarity, I knew—I had survived the storm, and now, I was walking toward the sun.

"New beginnings." That's what I called it.

I started focusing on the woman I had become. The strength I had cultivated through hardship. The resilience that had been quietly building inside me for years. I looked at my daughters and saw not just the future, but the reason I had fought so hard. I knew now that I didn't just survive—I transformed.

And I was ready for whatever came next.

Part 3:

The Irish Stranger

Chapter 13:

I never imagined that opening my home to international students would change my life so deeply. It began as a practical decision—a way to earn a little extra income while doing something meaningful. But from the moment I welcomed my first student at the door, suitcase in hand and eyes wide with both hope and nervousness, I knew this was going to be more than just a financial arrangement.

Becoming a host mum was like unlocking a new world right inside my own home. Our dinner table, once quiet and predictable, became a lively place filled with stories, laughter, and the comforting aroma of meals shared between strangers who quickly became family. With every student that arrived, a new chapter began—not just for them, but for me and my daughters as well.

I didn't just offer them a bed to sleep in—I gave them a space where they could exhale, be themselves, and feel part of something. I helped them navigate homesickness, decode assignment instructions, and settle into a country that was often colder, louder, or simply unfamiliar. And in return, they taught us about perseverance, joy, and cultures that stretched our understanding of the world far beyond our living room walls.

There were challenges, of course. There were moments of exhaustion and days when patience wore thin. But each challenge only deepened my commitment. My daughters, too, grew in ways I hadn't expected—they became more compassionate, more curious, and deeply connected to the idea of an "international family."

It had been a long, draining week. So, when my colleague suggested a night out to unwind, I didn't hesitate. We needed it—just a few hours to forget about responsibilities, dance, and feel like ourselves again. The nightclub we chose buzzed with life, the kind of place where the music wraps around you and you stop thinking for a while.

That night, I wasn't looking for anything. I just wanted to breathe.

Then I met him—Kelvin. An Irish man with a cheeky smile and kind eyes that somehow made me feel seen, even in the middle of all that noise.

It was a Friday night at a dim, slightly crowded bar tucked into a side street. The kind of place with worn leather booths, sticky floors, and music just loud enough to make you lean in a little closer. Neon lights buzzed faintly above the shelves of liquor bottles, and the scent of spilt beer and cheap perfume lingered in the air.

I wasn't planning on talking to anyone. I had come with a friend, halfheartedly sipping a rum and coke, trying to keep the week's weight off my face. Then Kelvin sat next to me at the bar, all tousled hair and easy presence.

"Is this seat taken?" he asked, nodding to the empty stool beside me.

I shook my head, barely looking up.

He sat, ordered a pint, and said with a grin, "You look like you're carrying a whole novel in your eyes."

I raised an eyebrow, caught off guard. "That's one way to start a conversation."

He laughed, the kind of laugh that softened everything around it. "Sorry, I'm usually smoother after a beer."

Our conversation started like any other—light, polite, maybe even forgettable. But it didn't stay that way. There was something about him. Maybe it was his easy laugh, or the way he genuinely listened when I spoke. He didn't interrupt. He didn't fill silences with noise. He just… paid attention.

Kelvin was a backpacker, passing through Australia with nothing but a rucksack and that disarming charm. He told me he was an environmental scientist—said it almost shyly, like he wasn't used to talking about himself.

"I was up north last week," he said, holding his pint glass between both hands. "Helping with a coastal erosion project. Lot of sand, wind, and… well, not much glamour."

I noticed the dirt under his fingernails and the tan lines on his wrists. He belonged to the earth in a way most people never really do.

And yet, he felt quietly rooted in mine—just for a moment.

We didn't plan it. One moment we were laughing over the strange names on the cocktail menu—"Bloody Fairy" still makes me smile—and the next, there was this pause. That kind of pause that doesn't feel awkward, just... full. Like the world had tilted slightly and given us a quiet space to notice each other differently.

His eyes lingered on mine, and I felt it. The shift.

Kelvin tilted his head, half-grinning. "You've got this little crease between your eyebrows when you're thinking. It's serious business."

I laughed, flustered. "You're staring."

He shrugged. "I know. I like watching you think."

And then—just like that—we kissed.

It caught me completely off guard. There was no lead-up, no dramatic music, no cliché. Just the closeness of the moment, the soft hum of a slow song playing in the background, and the sudden stillness that made everything else blur. His lips were warm, careful at first, like he was asking a question.

That kiss wasn't just about attraction—it was the warmth of being understood. The comfort of not needing to explain yourself. It was the surprise of connection when you're not even sure you were looking for one.

And for a moment, right there in that noisy, sticky-floor bar strangely, the world felt quiet.

I felt butterflies, real ones—the kind I hadn't felt in a long time. There was a lightness in me I didn't realize I'd been missing.

Before we parted ways, we exchanged numbers. I held my phone like it might tell me the future. Walking away from the club that night, I felt something I hadn't in a while: a little thrill, a little hope… and a smile I couldn't quite shake off.

The next morning, my phone buzzed with a message that made me smile before I'd even opened my eyes.

"How are you, little hottie?"
Cheeky. Playful. So, *him*, already.

I laughed quietly to myself, lying there in bed, still a little stunned by how one spontaneous night could stir up something so unexpected. There was a warmth behind his words—not just flirtation, but something familiar, like we'd known each other longer than just one night.

It was a crisp Saturday morning, the kind that practically invites you outside. Kelvin suggested we meet up again, this time in the daylight, away from the pulsing music and flashing lights. I felt that flutter of nerves in my chest—the kind that makes you question everything and yet still say *yes* without hesitation.

When we finally met, it was different—but in the best possible way. There was no awkwardness, no forced conversation. It just *felt* right. Kelvin was as affectionate and confident as he'd been the night before, but now I could see another side of him—thoughtful, attentive, grounded.

We walked, we talked, and I kept catching myself smiling for no reason at all. The ease between us was undeniable, like our connection hadn't been left behind in the nightclub but had simply followed us into the morning light. And in that moment, I knew this wasn't just a fleeting spark—it was something worth leaning into.

In those early days, Kelvin's presence slipped quietly into my life like a warm breeze—unassuming but deeply comforting. What started as flirty texts and weekend meetups soon became a steady rhythm I came to rely on. He had a way of showing up, not just in person, but emotionally—especially when I needed it most.

I was going through a rough patch, one of those stretches where everything feels a little too heavy and you start to doubt your own footing. But there he was—steadfast, kind, and somehow always knowing exactly when to say the right thing. His support helped me find my footing again.

With him, I laughed more. I smiled more. I remembered who I was.

I still recall one message he sent during a rushed lunch break at work. I was sitting outside, sandwich in hand, watching kids play in the distance, when my phone lit up with a simple:
"Just thinking about you. You're doing great, don't forget that."
It hit me harder than I expected—because someone *saw* me, really saw me, in the middle of my chaos.

But even as we grew closer, there was always a quiet awareness tucked in the back of my mind—that this wasn't forever. He'd told me early on that his time in Australia was temporary. Still, nothing quite prepares you for the moment the end arrives.

He told me he was heading back to Ireland, and asked if I'd be willing to see him off at Sydney Airport. My heart sank, but I didn't hesitate. It wasn't just about saying goodbye—it was about showing him what his presence had meant to me. Flying to Sydney felt like the most natural way to honor that.

When I walked into the terminal and saw him waiting, his face broke into that familiar smile—the one that had brightened so many of my days. In that moment, any doubt I had about coming disappeared. We didn't say much right away. We didn't need to. Being there was enough. It was my way of saying *thank you*—for the light he brought, for the confidence he helped me rediscover, and for reminding me that even brief connections can leave lasting marks on the heart.

A quick goodbye didn't feel right. Not for him. Not for *us*. I couldn't bear the thought of just texting a farewell or standing awkwardly at the departure gate, trying to find the right words in a crowded terminal with time running out. So, I booked a flight to Sydney.

It wasn't just about saying goodbye—it was about showing up for someone who had shown up for me. I wanted Kelvin to know that he mattered. That what we shared, even if fleeting, was real.

When I arrived at the airport and saw him waiting, everything else faded. His face lit up the second our eyes met, and for a moment, it felt like the chaos of the terminal just paused around us. I could tell he hadn't expected me to come, but the way his smile softened, the way he pulled me into a hug that lingered—it told me I'd made the right choice.

Instead of heading straight to goodbyes, we turned the day into something beautiful. A small escape. One last adventure together. We wandered the city like two people trying to hold on to borrowed time. We stood side by side at the Opera House, silently taking in the view, neither of us needing to fill the quiet. At the museum, we pointed out strange exhibits and laughed like kids. We rode the monorail, visited the parks, and shared stories as if we had all the time in the world—even though we both knew we didn't.

And when the sun dipped below the skyline, painting the city in soft gold, we found ourselves in a nightclub again—full circle from the night we first met. But this time, everything was different. We weren't strangers dancing through chance—we were two people holding on. I remember the music surrounding us, but all I really noticed was the way he looked at me. Like he was memorizing me. Like he didn't want to forget.

We danced until our legs ached, until we were laughing breathlessly. And then, just like that, the night began to settle. We walked back to the motel quietly, not because we had nothing to say, but because there was nothing that needed saying. Every touch of his hand, every glance, every pause—it said everything.

Lying beside him that night, tangled in the sheets and the silence, I tried to soak it all in. The warmth of his body next to mine, the sound of his breathing slowing, the way his arm pulled me just a little closer as we drifted off. There was a softness in that moment, the kind that aches even as it comforts. I knew this would be the last time I'd fall asleep beside him, and that knowledge sat heavy in my chest—but I held on anyway.

Because even though it was ending, what we had deserved to be felt fully.

Chapter 14:

The morning air at Darling Harbor carried a certain stillness, the kind that usually feels peaceful. But not that day. That day, it felt eerie—like the world was holding its breath. I wandered past shopfronts and cafés, trying to hold onto the lightness from the night before. But something was wrong. Deeply wrong.

I reached for my phone to send Kelvin a message, but my fingers wouldn't close around it. My hand… it wasn't moving.

At first, I stared at it, willing myself not to panic. *Maybe I slept on it funny,* I thought, shaking it out, trying to jolt it back to life. Nothing. No tingling, no pins and needles. Just an unnerving, icy numbness creeping up my arm. I held it up to my chest, trying not to cry in the middle of the street.

My mind raced. *What is this? Why can't I move it?* Every step I took felt heavier, as if my body was turning against me. Fear twisted in my stomach. I needed to get back. I needed *him.*

I don't remember the walk back to the motel, only that I was trembling when I reached the door. When Kelvin opened it, the worry on his face hit me like a wave. His eyes scanned me quickly, like he was checking for damage.

"My hand," I choked out, tears brimming. "It's not working—I can't feel anything."

He didn't hesitate. He didn't ask a dozen questions. He simply took me by the arm and said, "We're going to the hospital. Now."

We barely spoke on the ride there. I was gripping his hand with the one that still worked, trying to hold onto something real—trying not to spiral. My thoughts were frantic. *Was it a stroke? A pinched nerve? Something worse?* And through it all, Kelvin stayed calm—his thumb gently rubbing circles against my knuckles. Like he knew I was one breath away from falling apart.

When we reached the hospital, the fluorescent lights and antiseptic scent hit me all at once. My knees buckled.

Then everything blurred.

I heard myself gasp, felt the ground come up fast. And then—nothing.

Black.

In the chaos, I caught flashes—Kelvin yelling for help, his voice panicked and sharp. "She collapsed! Help! She needs help now!"
I was drifting, the world distant and underwater, but I clung to the sound of his voice like a lifeline.

He ran through the corridors, frantic, calling for nurses, doctors—anyone. I wasn't just someone he met in a nightclub anymore. I was someone he *cared* about. And that made everything sharper—the pain, the fear, the not knowing.

When I came to—only briefly—I saw him leaning over me, eyes wide with fear, whispering, "Stay with me. Please, just stay."

I could barely respond, but I remember feeling safe, even as the world around me spun out of control. Because he was there. And somehow, in the middle of the most terrifying moment of my life… that meant everything.

When I opened my eyes, the world was no longer familiar.

I was cocooned in the sterile stillness of the ICU, the soft glow of monitors blinking around me like distant stars. The steady *beep… beep… beep* of machines echoed through the room, keeping time with a heart that felt like it didn't quite belong to me anymore. My mind was foggy. Disoriented. My cheeks were wet, though I hadn't realized I was crying.

And then the reality hit me: I couldn't speak.

There was a tube down my throat, silencing me. No words. No sounds. Just a choking frustration pressing on my chest, trapped beneath the surface of everything I wanted to scream. I tried to move, to sit up—to *do something*—but my body betrayed me. I felt heavy, like gravity had doubled its grip on me. And then, the true horror settled in.

The entire left side of my body… was lifeless.

I couldn't feel it. Couldn't move it. It was as if half of me had disappeared.

Panic surged, but in that sea of confusion, I heard a voice— familiar, soft, trembling with tenderness.

"Open your pretty little eyes."

It was Kelvin.

His words were like a rope tossed into the depths, pulling me back to the surface. I blinked again, forcing my vision to focus. There he was, hovering close, eyes rimmed with exhaustion and worry. I couldn't speak, but I reached for him with the only strength I had left. I squeezed his thumb—a tiny, desperate plea: *Don't leave me.*

His eyes closed for a moment, as if holding back a wave of emotion. "I don't want to go," he whispered. "But I have to."

His voice broke slightly.

He was leaving. His work in Australia was done. As an environmental scientist, he had to return to Ireland. He had stayed longer than planned. But now, duty called.

I couldn't say a word. Only feel. And it *hurt*—not just in my paralyzed limbs, but in my heart.

He kissed my forehead and whispered goodbye.

I wanted to believe we were more than a passing moment. But the question clawed at me as I lay there, unable to follow him, unable to move, unable to speak.

Was it just a beautiful chapter, now closed?

For ten days, I existed in that suspended, fragile space between life and healing. Time stretched and folded around me. I watched nurses come and go, felt the sting of fear every time a doctor approached my bedside with updates, and clung to every visit from my daughters.

Hearing their voices—*my girls*—brought tears to my eyes. Even in my weakness, I felt their strength. They were my light, my reason to fight. And seeing them there—bonded, strong, tender with one another—filled me with a quiet, aching gratitude.

But the emotions were too much.

My blood pressure soared. The machines shrieked. Nurses came running, trying to stabilize the storm inside me. I wanted to tell them, *It's not pain, it's love. It's fear. It's all too much.* But I couldn't say a word.

Eventually, the doctors decided to move me closer to home—to a specialized rehabilitation hospital. It was a critical transfer, and the only way to get there was by helicopter. As I was lifted onto the stretcher, bundled in blankets, I looked at the sky. For the first time in days, I felt the sun.

It was a harsh awakening, yes—but also a reminder.

I was still alive.

And life, in all its terrifying fragility, was still mine to live.

Chapter 15:

Treatment began with quiet urgency. Every day brought new faces—doctors evaluating, nurses monitoring, therapists mapping out the road ahead. The clinical routines felt overwhelming, but what grounded me in those early days was the invisible thread of love—his love—that still tethered me to hope. Though Kelvin was far away, his presence lingered in the small, meaningful ways that reached across oceans.

Red roses arrived first. Then, a soft teddy bear—warm and worn, as if it had already held the weight of sleepless nights. There was a sympathy card too, not sombre, but sincere. Inside were his words, careful and full of feeling: "You are the strongest person I know. Keep going. I'm with you, always." Those words became my lifeline.

They wrapped around me on the days I broke down, when I cried without understanding why. When tears streamed in silence, and I stared out the hospital window trying to piece together this new version of myself. My body had changed. My life had changed. And somewhere inside, so had my mind.

Then came the conversation that broke me. My occupational therapist sat down beside me; her voice soft but firm. "Your left hand," she said gently, "is not going to regain full function."

At first, I didn't believe her. It felt surreal—like a plot twist in someone else's story, not mine. I stared at my hand, willing it to move, willing it to prove her wrong. But nothing happened. Denial morphed into shock, and then grief came crashing in like a wave. I mourned not just the limb, but the woman I had been—the ease, the independence, the normalcy.

Coping with that reality was an emotional storm. Some days I sobbed quietly into my pillow. Other days I forced a smile and nodded politely, even when I felt like screaming inside. But every step forward—no matter how painful— was also a lesson in letting go.

And then, there was a different kind of pain. My mother did not visit me when I was in the ICU.
Not when I was unconscious. Not when my life hung in the balance. She didn't come—not because she couldn't, but because she chose not to.

She wanted my half-brother to come to Australia instead— because he had never been here before. That was her reason. Not her daughter in a life-and-death situation. Not the child she gave birth to. But the son she raised.

I tried to understand it. I tried to make peace with it. But truthfully—it hurt me. It scarred me. For life. How can a mother not come to see her daughter in the ICU? How can she choose absence over comfort, distance over presence— at the most critical moment? Maybe because she didn't raise me.
Maybe because I was never hers in the way I needed her to be.
But that knowledge didn't make it hurt any less.

In the walls of rehab, I didn't just learn to walk again—I learned how to live again.
There were days I celebrated the smallest victories, like buttoning my shirt or lifting a fork.
And then, without warning, life pulled the ground from beneath me once more.

Coming home after three months in rehab should have felt like a victory. And in many ways, it was. I'd survived. I'd made it through the worst. But walking—or rather, being wheeled—through the front door, I realized that survival was just the beginning. Recovery would take a village. And in my case, that village was led by a sixteen-year-old girl.

Cassie—my youngest—became my anchor. While other girls her age were worrying about exams, part-time jobs, or weekend plans, mine was learning how to care for a mother who could no longer dress herself.

She showered me when I couldn't lift my arms. She helped me into bed, made sure I ate lunch before heading off to university, and always reminded me to stay strong—even when her own eyes looked heavy with the weight of responsibility.

She had no choice but to grow up fast. Sixteen going on thirty.

When I think back to those early days, what I remember most is her quiet steadiness. The way she'd brush my hair and say, "You're doing great, Mum," even when I wasn't. How she'd drive me to doctors' appointments, physio sessions, urgent care—never once complaining, never once making me feel like a burden.

And while Cassie became my daily lifeline, Natasha—my eldest—carried her own heavy load. She was studying and working full time, balancing textbooks and shifts with the quiet ache of watching her mother struggle. She didn't have hours to spare, but when she came, she came with warmth and calm, always asking, "What do you need, Mum?" before I could even answer.

They were my daughters. But in that chapter, they became my caregivers, my strength, my home.
I will never forget the love they gave me when I had nothing left to give myself.

Kelvin lived in Ireland, and during the months I was in hospital, we couldn't speak directly. But after I returned home—three months later—we reconnected over Skype. I still remember the moment his face appeared on the screen, his eyes full of warmth and worry. He didn't flinch at my changed appearance. He didn't ask awkward questions. He just looked at me, smiled softly, and said, "There you are." And somehow, in that small square of a screen, I felt seen again.

His support never wavered. Each message, each call, felt like a gentle hand on my back, nudging me forward. He reminded me of who I was beneath the injury—strong, vibrant, deeply alive.

I surrendered myself to the hospital team, letting their expertise and compassion carry me through. I had to trust them. I had to trust myself. And slowly, something unexpected began to grow in me.

There were days I laughed—real laughter, surprised and spontaneous. There were nights I prayed, not always for healing, but for peace.
I realized that healing wasn't just physical. It was emotional. It was spiritual. It was the way I began to see beauty again—even in the broken parts.

Seven years.
Seven years of love that stood by me like a lighthouse through storm after storm. Kelvin, with his steady heart, and my daughters, with their quiet strength, were the pillars

that held me up when I didn't even recognize myself anymore. They loved me when I couldn't love what I saw in the mirror. They reminded me who I was when I had forgotten.

Chapter: 16

My mother died.
And I couldn't go home to bury her.

The doctors told me I couldn't fly. The air pressure on the plane could reopen the stitches in my brain. It wasn't safe—there was no discussion. My body, still fragile from surgery and trauma, wasn't strong enough for the journey. So, I stayed behind. Not by choice, but by necessity.

And while I lay in bed, staring at the ceiling, my mother was lowered into the ground on the other side of the world.

No final embrace.
No whispered goodbye.
No funeral. Just absence—and a silence that roared louder than anything I'd ever heard.

There was pain, yes—but also something deeper, more difficult to name. It wasn't just grief. It was a quiet, aching hollowness. A question with no answer.

Even after everything—even after she hadn't come to see me when I was in the ICU, even after I'd told myself I didn't need her anymore—I still wanted to be there for her. Some part of me still needed that goodbye. Still wanted to say: *I was here. I was your daughter. I tried.*

But I never got the chance.

We had always lived with distance—emotional, physical, historical. She didn't raise me. She wasn't a constant presence in my life. And yet, there's something about a mother's death that brings everything to the surface. All the old hopes. All the unfinished conversations. All the versions of love that were never spoken aloud.

I lit a candle beside my bed. That's all I could do. A small, flickering flame in a quiet room, meant to honor a lifetime of complicated love.

Grief settled into me—not loud, but heavy. It wasn't just about her absence now. It was about every absence that had come before. Every time I had longed for her. Every time I had wished things were different. And now there would be no change. No mending. Just what was. And what would never be.

They say grief has stages.
But mine felt more like circles—looping back through memory, regret, sorrow, and something close to peace.

I couldn't go to her funeral. But in that moment, I carried her. Not in flowers or rituals, but in memory. In truth. In the complicated, tangled bond that never broke—even when we did.

I turned to God—not just to ask for healing, but to surrender. I was done pretending I had it all together. I had seizures. I had scars. I had days when I cried until there was nothing left. But in my weakest moments, I felt something deeper. A presence. A strength I couldn't explain.
God carried me when my own legs couldn't.

I stopped trying to hold everything by myself. I let the prayers rise—not polished ones, not perfect ones. Just raw, honest words whispered in the dark: *Help me. Heal me. Hold me.* And somehow, I felt heard. Not always answered the way I wanted—but never alone.

Faith became my oxygen. On the days when grief suffocated me, when pain wrapped tight around my chest, I would close my eyes and just breathe His name. That was enough. Sometimes, that was everything.

God didn't erase the hardship. But He gave me the courage to face it. The grace to keep going. And the quiet reassurance that even broken things can still be held—beautifully, gently, completely.

I wore an orthotic in my shoe. My arm rested in a collar and cuff. I leaned on a walking stick. Every day was a challenge. Every movement, a deliberate act of courage. Simple things—tying shoelaces, lifting a pot, opening a door—became small mountains.

But I climbed them.

Stepping out into the world, though, brought a new kind of pain. People stared. Not out of cruelty, but curiosity. Pity. Confusion. Their eyes said everything they didn't dare speak. And each glance cut like glass.

Still, I smiled.

Because I had learned something: smiles are armor. Smiles are bridges. When I smiled back, something shifted. Their gaze softened. Strangers became human again. Some smiled too. In that moment, we weren't broken or perfect. We were just people, trying.

I whispered affirmations under my breath like prayers: I am strong. I am capable. I am worthy.

And over time, I believed them.

I emerged from the ashes of my old life not as the woman I once was—but as someone wiser, deeper, softer in the ways that mattered.

This is my new chapter.

I still go to therapy. I still stumble. I still cry. But I also laugh louder. I love harder. And I *live* more deeply than I ever did before.

I live independently now—not just in body, but in spirit. I make my own choices. I lead my own healing. I am free.

And through it all, one truth has never changed: Family is everything.

Not just the people who share your blood, but those who hold your hand in the dark and whisper, *"You've got this."*

There were moments in my life when I truly felt alone. My parents were oceans away in Fiji—emotionally distant, unavailable, and unable to offer the support I so desperately needed. In Australia, I had no extended family, no one to lean on when the weight of my world began to collapse.

But I had *them*. My daughters.

They were my reason. My light. My motivation to keep going when everything inside me wanted to give up. Their laughter, their tiny hands, their innocent questions—those were the lifelines that pulled me out of despair, day after day.

They were so young, far too young to understand the magnitude of what was happening around them. And yet, they adapted. They showed a kind of quiet bravery that still leaves me in awe. I wanted nothing more than to give them stability, a sense of home, a thread of normalcy in a life that had become unpredictable.

I pushed down my pain. Suppressed my fear.
Because that's what mothers do.

Chapter 17:

Rehab was filled with milestones—first steps, first twitches, first moments of hope. But some of the hardest healing happened in silence. In moments where there were no therapists, no exercises, just the quiet ache of what was slipping away.

Kelvin waited. Even across oceans and time zones, he waited.

He called often—his voice still filled with warmth, still asking how I was doing before I even had the strength to answer. And with every call, I felt the pull—the sweetness of a love that hadn't faltered, that believed in me even when I didn't recognize myself.

But something had changed.

Not in him. In me.

My arms had stopped working. My nerves were failing me. I was relearning how to live in a body that had betrayed me. And somewhere deep inside, I knew—I couldn't hold him the way he deserved. I couldn't give him a future filled with spontaneity or certainty. And he would never ask me to. But still—I couldn't let him carry this weight.

The day I made the call, I felt like I was breaking my own heart.

He picked up after the second ring.

"Hey, love," he said, his voice soft and familiar. "I've been thinking about you all day."

I closed my eyes, already fighting tears. "Kelvin…"

Something in my voice made him pause. "What is it?"

"I need to say something, and I need you to let me finish."

The line went quiet. "Alright."

"I love you," I said, the words falling out like broken glass. "And that's why I have to let you go."

"No," he said, quickly. "Don't say that. Don't—"

"I can't ask you to keep waiting. I can't ask you to keep loving someone who may never hold you again the way she wants to. Who may never walk beside you without stumbling. Who wakes up some mornings and feels like half of her is gone."

"Stop," he whispered, but his voice cracked. "You don't get to decide how much I love you."

"I'm deciding because I have to," I replied, barely holding back sobs. "You deserve a life that's full, not one that revolves around hospital beds and broken promises."

"You were never a broken promise," he said, pain threading through every word. "You were the only thing that made sense."

Silence filled the space between us. And then I said the hardest thing I've ever said.

"Goodbye, Kelvin."

There was a pause—just long enough to hear him break.

"I would've waited forever," he said. "But I won't stop loving you. Not even now."

Then the line went dead.

And all I could do was cry. Not because I regretted it—but because sometimes, love means letting go. Not for yourself, but for them.

And I let him go, not because he wasn't perfect—but because he was.

Part 4:

The One Who Fooled Me

Chapter 18:

In the thick of exhaustion and stress, during that turbulent time, I met someone new.

I met Matthew through my aunt, at a time when I was already stretched thin—emotionally, financially, in every possible way. He seemed… safe. Calm. The kind of person who didn't raise his voice, who smiled softly and asked questions instead of making statements.

"I know what it's like to lose your footing," he said one afternoon over tea at my aunt's. "If I can help in any way, I will."

He'd lost his wife not long before. He had children, a life, a house of his own. I never thought he was trying to start something romantic. That was never on the table. We were just two people—mutually trying to find stability. That's how he made it sound.

So, when he suggested buying a house together—fifty-fifty—I thought it was a strange kind of generosity, but not unwelcome. "You can live in it," he said. "You need it more than I do. I'm mostly up north for work anyway."

It wasn't love. It was survival.

I moved in. Made the house a home. For three years, I lived there alone, tending to the garden, folding laundry in the living room, trying to piece myself together in a space that finally felt mine. He stayed in his own home with his kids, came by rarely, just enough to remind me he existed on paper.

One day, living alone, I was thrust into one of the most terrifying and vulnerable experiences of my life. Without warning, my body betrayed me—my brain misfired, and I collapsed onto the floor. I couldn't move. My limbs refused to respond, and tears slipped down my face as I lay there, helpless and shaking. It was more than fear—it was the raw, terrifying realization of how fragile and powerful the brain truly is. In that moment, I gained a newfound respect for the mind's quiet command over the body.

Just before the seizure overtook me, some instinct kicked in—a final spark of clarity—and I managed to make an urgent call. That action, though small, set everything in motion. My daughters were alerted immediately.

For them, it was a nightmare. By the time they arrived at the hospital, I was unconscious, unreachable. I can only imagine the fear that gripped them as they stood by my side, unsure of what would happen next. But they didn't waver. Their quick thinking and fierce love became my lifeline.

Though I couldn't speak or open my eyes, I felt the weight of their presence—their strength, their care, their refusal to give in to panic. In the aftermath, as I pieced together what had happened, I was overwhelmed with gratitude. Knowing they were there, holding me in their thoughts and in their hands, gave me a profound sense of comfort. Even in my most fragile state, I wasn't alone.

When I regained consciousness in the hospital, I was enveloped by a fog of confusion. I had no memory of how I'd gotten there, and the disorientation only deepened my fear and anxiety. The sterile smell, the rhythmic beeping of machines, the unfamiliar voices around me—it all felt surreal, like waking up in someone else's life. I was vulnerable, exposed, and utterly unmoored.

Despite the unease, I was aware—beneath the surface—of an immense gratitude for the care I was receiving. I knew I was safe, even if my body and mind were slow to catch up.

At one point, in the grip of sedation and blurred reality, I became convinced I was restrained, trapped in a bed I couldn't escape. Panic surged. I felt stripped of my autonomy, my dignity. In that moment of fear and confusion, I lashed out at the nurses—swearing, shouting, desperately expressing a need for control, for freedom. My words were raw and unfiltered, born not from who I am, but from what I was enduring. Still, they stung in hindsight.

The next morning, as the haze lifted and clarity returned, so did a deep sense of shame. I remembered the way I had spoken, and my heart sank. I felt exposed—not just physically, but emotionally. With sincerity, I apologized to the medical staff, trying to convey the regret that weighed heavily on me. I wanted them to know that wasn't me—not truly.

To my relief, their response was filled with kindness. The doctors explained that the combination of medication and trauma could distort behavior, that my actions weren't uncommon in such circumstances. Their compassion allowed me to breathe a little easier. It reminded me that being human includes moments of weakness, and that forgiveness—especially of oneself—is part of healing too.

That experience, as disorienting as it was, marked a turning point. I wasn't just recovering physically—I was learning to extend grace to myself, even when I stumbled.

After several intense days in the ICU, I was finally moved to a regular ward—a quiet but meaningful milestone in my recovery. It felt like a small victory, a sign that my condition was stabilizing. That transition brought with it a glimmer of hope, a whisper that healing was possible even after such a frightening ordeal.

I spent six days in the hospital in total before I was discharged and placed under outpatient care. Walking—or rather, being wheeled—out of that building felt symbolic. I wasn't just leaving a hospital; I was stepping into a new chapter; one filled with both uncertainty and determination. Despite the shadows that still lingered, I was filled with a cautious optimism. I wanted to believe that this marked the beginning of better health, of reclaiming control over my life.

But recovery is rarely linear.

Soon after returning home, I began to notice a weakness along one side of my body—a persistent, unnerving imbalance that made everyday tasks feel unfamiliar. It wasn't just fatigue; it was something deeper, a quiet warning that neurological or muscular complications might still be unfolding. Each time I tried to grip something, stand steadily, or move with confidence, I was reminded that I had a long road ahead.

Still, I didn't see it as defeat. It was a sobering realization, yes—but also a call to remain patient, resilient, and fiercely committed to my healing. Each step, no matter how small or shaky, was progress. And progress, I reminded myself, was still a form of strength.

The next morning, I had an important conversation with the neurologist—one that I didn't realize I needed as much as I did. Sitting there, still tired and fragile, I found myself opening up in a way I hadn't before. I told him about the days leading up to the seizure—the constant movement, the endless to-do lists, the way I kept pushing myself around the house, trying to stay on top of everything. Cooking, cleaning, managing it all like I always had. But this time, it was too much.

As I spoke, it hit me just how much I had been carrying. How I'd been ignoring the quiet signs that my body was trying to send me. It felt like a relief just to say it out loud. To admit that I'd been running on empty, pretending I was fine when I wasn't.

The neurologist listened patiently. He gently explained how the brain, under too much stress—physical, emotional, or both—can sometimes just shut down. Not as punishment, but as protection. As if my body had reached its limit and pulled the brakes for me when I wouldn't do it myself.

That moment stayed with me. It wasn't just about understanding what caused the seizure—it was about seeing myself with a little more compassion. Realizing that strength doesn't mean doing everything on your own. Sometimes, it means slowing down. Letting go. Taking care of yourself before everything falls apart.

That conversation planted a seed. It reminded me that I matter too—not just the chores, the responsibilities, the appearances. Me. And from that day on, I promised myself I'd start listening a little closer to the quiet signals, and honor them, before they had to scream.

Chapter 19:

Matthew came into my life like a white knight, or so I thought. I wanted to believe in his kindness, to believe that someone could show up without expecting something in return. But that illusion shattered quickly. His support wasn't generosity—it was leverage. And the price he expected for his "help" wasn't interest or repayment. It was my body.

He came over unexpectedly, standing in the doorway like a shadow.

"I've been thinking," he said, not even bothering to sit down. "About the house. About us."

I looked up from the couch, confused. "Okay… what about it?"

"This isn't really working anymore."

"What do you mean? I've been paying my half. You've been paying yours. What's not working?"

He took a step closer, his voice cooler now. "You're living in a house I'm paying for, and we're not even... together. Not really."

A strange coldness crept up my spine.

"What are you trying to say, Matthew?"

"I think it's only fair," he said slowly, "that if I'm going to keep paying into something I don't use, I get something in return."

The words didn't hit me all at once. They hovered. Hung in the room like cigarette smoke.

"I don't understand," I said, though part of me already did.

He met my eyes without blinking. "I'm saying... we could be in a real relationship. A proper one. You and me. That way, it all makes sense."

A knot formed in my stomach.

"A real relationship," I echoed. "Or sex?"

He didn't answer. Just tilted his head slightly. Shrugged. Like it didn't matter.

What he proposed wasn't a partnership. It was a transaction. A quiet, calculated expectation that I would trade my dignity for a loan. The realization hit me like a punch to the chest. I wasn't being helped—I was being cornered, reduced to something to be bought, manipulated, owned.

"I never agreed to this," I said, my voice starting to shake. "This was never part of the deal."

He stepped back slightly, folding his arms. "Then I'll stop paying. Simple as that."

"You said this was to help me. That it was about stability, not conditions."

"Stability comes at a cost," he said flatly. "I've done my part."

I felt sick. Not just at him, but at myself—for not seeing it sooner, for trusting him even a little. The thought that he had looked at my vulnerability and seen opportunity—that my desperation had made me a target—filled me with a kind of rage I hadn't known I was capable of. It made my skin crawl. It made my soul ache.

I was already struggling. Menopause had left me feeling like a stranger in my own body—exhausted, moody, unsteady. I was fighting to hold onto pieces of myself, and now this man wanted to take what was left. To twist my need into something shameful.

I couldn't breathe. My skin burned. The walls that once felt warm now felt like they were closing in. I looked around at the house I'd cared for—swept, painted, made into a home—and suddenly it all felt like a trap.

"You used me," I whispered. "You never cared about helping me. You just waited. You waited until you thought I had no choice."

He didn't deny it. That was the worst part.

It took everything I had to look him in the eye and say no— to tell him I would rather lose everything than give in to that kind of exploitation. My voice trembled, but it didn't break. That moment wasn't just a boundary—it was a battle cry. I was reclaiming myself. I was saying: You don't get to own me. Not for money. Not for anything.

He followed through. Cold and mechanical. Just business. He stopped paying his share of the mortgage. Put the house up for sale. Told me plainly:

"If you don't move out, the bank will take it. You'll lose everything anyway."

I had no choice.

I packed my things in silence. Every box was a wound. Every step out of that house was a step away from a lie I thought had been safety.

It wasn't just the house I lost.

It was the illusion that anyone had ever wanted to help me without a price.

In moments of stillness, I questioned whether my open heart was a gift or a weakness. It's hard not to feel exposed in a world that sometimes rewards the cunning over the kind. I wasn't naive—I just believed in people, and maybe that belief came at a cost.

He mistook my vulnerability for weakness. He didn't see the fire underneath.

Chapter 20:

Supporting my daughters during a difficult chapter in their lives became one of the most meaningful and healing experiences for me. After everything I had been through, being able to show up for them—not just as their mother, but as a steady presence—brought a deep sense of joy and purpose. Even in the middle of my own healing, I found strength in being there for them. It reminded me that love has a way of expanding, even when we feel stretched thin.

During this time, I also received long-term support from the Australian government, and I can't overstate how much that meant to me. It gave me something I hadn't felt in a long time: stability. Knowing that I had consistent help took an enormous weight off my shoulders. I could finally breathe without constantly worrying about how I'd make it through the next week. It gave me the space I needed to rebuild—not just my life, but my spirit too.

For the first time in a long while, I felt like I wasn't doing it all alone. And that mattered more than words can say. The support wasn't just financial—it was a reminder that it's okay to lean on others. That accepting help doesn't make you weak; it gives you the foundation to grow stronger.

This chapter of my life taught me so much about resilience—not the loud, heroic kind, but the quiet kind. The kind that shows up in everyday choices, in the willingness to keep going, and in the grace to ask for help when you need it. I'm deeply grateful to the Australian government for offering that safety net when I needed it most. Their support helped me find my footing again—and for that, I carry a lasting sense of gratitude.

One of the hardest changes I had to face was losing my driver's license. It wasn't just about not being able to drive—it was about what driving had always meant to me: freedom, independence, and control over my own life. Having that taken away because of my ongoing seizures felt like a sharp blow to my confidence. I tried to reclaim that independence by retaking my driving test, but I failed. My brain, still healing, couldn't send clear signals to the left side of my body. I felt betrayed by my own body, frustrated by the limits I didn't want to accept.

But in that disappointment, something shifted. I stopped fighting reality and started listening to it. Failing the test became a moment of clarity—not of defeat, but of understanding. I began to see that protecting my health and safety mattered more than holding onto an old version of myself. It wasn't easy to let go, but it was necessary. And in that acceptance, I found a strange kind of peace.

Since I could no longer drive, I began to rely on my support workers for transportation. At first, I dreaded the dependence. But to my surprise, it became one of the most comforting parts of my routine. There was something tender in the way they cared for me—opening car doors, gently helping me in and out, even bringing an umbrella when the sky threatened rain. These gestures, so simple and thoughtful, made me feel cherished in a way I hadn't expected. I found myself smiling at moments I once would've resisted.

It was humbling, yes—but it was also beautiful. It reminded me that accepting help doesn't mean losing dignity. Sometimes, it means receiving love in its quietest, most genuine form. In those car rides and shared silences, I realized I wasn't just being transported—I was being cared for. And that, in its own way, made me feel like royalty.

The care and kindness I received during this time left me emotionally overwhelmed—in the best way. I had never experienced that level of thoughtful attention before, and it opened something in me. I wasn't just grateful; I was moved. Every small gesture, every word of reassurance, made me feel seen, valued, and deeply human. That kind of compassion changes you.

It stirred something inside me—a quiet but powerful urge to give back. I knew what it felt like to be vulnerable, to face limitations you never asked for, and to long for someone who truly understands. So, I began offering my time to others who were navigating similar injuries. I didn't have all the answers, but I had my story. And sometimes, that's enough.

I listened. I sat with people in their pain. I shared pieces of my own healing when it felt right. And in doing so, something beautiful happened. I found a renewed sense of purpose—not in fixing anyone, but in simply being there with empathy and understanding. Those connections became medicine for my own soul too.

Helping others reminded me that healing isn't just about regaining what was lost—it's also about discovering what still lives in you. I was no longer just surviving; I was contributing. And that, more than anything, made me feel whole again.

One of the most joyful and emotional moments during this season of my life was celebrating my older daughter's engagement to her high school sweetheart. Their love—so pure, so steady—was a beautiful reminder that even in life's hardest moments, something meaningful and enduring can take root. Watching them step into their future together filled my heart with an indescribable mix of pride, love, and awe.

As a mother, seeing my daughter grow into a strong, kind, and capable woman was both deeply fulfilling and a little bittersweet. I could still remember holding her tiny hand, tying her shoelaces, listening to her teenage dreams. And now, here she was—stepping into a lifelong commitment with grace and confidence. Part of me wanted to hold on just a little longer, to protect her from the world. But an even bigger part of me was bursting with pride, knowing she was exactly where she was meant to be.

Despite everything I was going through personally—my health, my limitations, the emotional weight of my journey—I made a conscious decision to be fully present. I stayed calm, centered, and intentional. I didn't want my challenges to overshadow their joy. Instead, I nurtured my energy and spirit so I could stand beside her, steady and supportive, as she walked into this new chapter.

This experience helped me realize just how vital calmness and inner peace have become in my life. It marked a turning point—a moment where I truly embraced a slower, more intentional way of living. And in that stillness, I discovered a deeper strength. Letting go of the fast-paced life I once led has been a journey in itself, but I've welcomed it with hope. The quiet has become a space for reflection, healing, and growth.

This new rhythm has shown me that even as roles shift— from caretaker to witness, from fixer to supporter—love doesn't lose its depth. It simply changes shape. And being there, truly there, for my daughter during one of the most meaningful times in her life... that will forever be one of my greatest honors as a mother.

Part 5:

From Ashes to Hope

Chapter 21:

When Matthew made it clear that his offer of a housing partnership came with an unspoken expectation of sex, I felt a wave of disbelief wash over me. The idea that my safety, stability, and shelter could be dangled as a bargaining chip for intimacy was both infuriating and heartbreaking. In that moment, I realized something vital: I had the right to say no.

No matter how vulnerable I felt, no matter how much I needed a roof over my head, I knew my dignity wasn't negotiable. Setting that boundary wasn't easy—it came with fear, uncertainty, and the looming question of where I would go next. But saying no wasn't just about rejecting him. It was about choosing myself. It was a declaration of worth, a refusal to be reduced to a transaction.

Walking away from that situation meant I had to start over again. I found myself back in a familiar place of uncertainty, this time without the safety net I had counted on. But strangely, there was a quiet strength in that choice. I wasn't running—I was standing tall, even while the ground beneath me shifted.

I didn't know where I would land, but I did know one thing: I would never compromise my self-respect to feel safe. I deserved more than that. We all do.

Just when I felt the weight of uncertainty pressing down on me, a lifeline appeared in the most unexpected way. A dear friend introduced me to her neighbour, Grant—a man whose quiet strength and gentle nature quickly became a source of comfort during a difficult transition.

Grant wasn't just generous—he was deeply good. A devoted son, he cared for his 90-year-old mother with unwavering patience and love. Though they lived in separate houses, his closeness to her, both in distance and in heart, spoke volumes about the kind of man he was. I was struck by his ability to balance independence with responsibility. I admired him deeply, not in a romantic sense, but as a rare soul whose kindness restored some of my faith in humanity.

Grant offered me the chance to rent two rooms in his spacious five-bedroom home—a gesture that meant far more than simply providing a roof over my head. It was stability, safety, and dignity at a time I needed it most. Moving in with Grant and getting to know his mother was surprisingly smooth. Their calm and steady rhythm gave me a sense of peace I hadn't felt in a long time.

My friend Jean, too, was a blessing. Her warmth, local knowledge, and the simplest gestures—like stopping by for tea and biscuits—reminded me that connection and kindness can turn a house into a home. Her presence made settling in feel less like starting over and more like finding a new chapter.

Grant's daily routine reflected his character—disciplined, humble, and hardworking. He rose before the sun, working long, grueling shifts at a concrete factory from 5 a.m. to 5 p.m., followed by a long commute. And still, he managed to show up—not just for his mother, but for those around him. In the evenings, he kept things simple: a quiet dinner, some TV, and an early night. We respected each other's space and routines, and that mutual understanding allowed our friendship to grow naturally, without pressure or expectation.

This unexpected arrangement became a refuge—not only physically, but emotionally. It was a gentle reminder that sometimes, the most healing places are not found in grand gestures, but in shared respect, quiet generosity, and the unexpected kindness of good people.

As the days turned into weeks, my friendship with Grant and Jean became an anchor in my healing journey. Their presence brought comfort during a time when I was still learning how to trust again—not just in people, but in life itself. They reminded me that not all relationships come with expectations or conditions. Some people simply care because that's who they are.

Grant's quiet, steady companionship was like a balm to my wounded spirit. He didn't pry or pressure. He was simply there—a constant, calming presence in the background. Whether it was the simple act of sharing a meal in silence or exchanging small talk at the end of a long day, those everyday moments built a sense of safety I hadn't realized I was missing. His kindness, his reliability, his ability to respect boundaries without question—those qualities became the quiet scaffolding that helped me rebuild my inner strength.

Jean, on the other hand, brought light into my life with her warmth and cheer. She had a way of knowing when I needed company and when I needed space. Her small, thoughtful gestures—like stopping by for tea or inviting me for a stroll—reminded me that healing doesn't always come in dramatic moments. Sometimes, it's in the laughter over biscuits, the shared stories, or simply sitting together in silence, knowing you're not alone.

The friendship I found in Grant and Jean was more than companionship—it was a lifeline. In their own ways, they helped me rediscover trust, compassion, and the deep value of human connection. They never asked for anything in return, and yet gave so much of themselves, proving that friendship can be one of the most powerful forms of medicine.

Through them, I learned that you don't have to go through pain alone. That in the presence of good people, it's okay to let your guard down. And that love and support, in their purest form, can come quietly—without drama, without expectation, but with a healing force stronger than I ever imagined.

Their friendship didn't just help me through—it helped me grow. It reminded me who I was beneath the scars, and showed me who I could still become.

Jean's kindness didn't stop at tea and thoughtful conversation—she remained a steadfast advocate for my well-being when I needed it most. When it came time to settle matters with Matthew's house sale, she took it upon herself to ensure I wasn't left behind or overlooked. With quiet determination and unwavering loyalty, she introduced me to her solicitor, someone she trusted, and helped prepare all the necessary documents.

I was overwhelmed—not just by the legal complexities, but by the emotional weight of it all. Yet Jean was right there beside me, guiding me through each step with patience and clarity. Thanks to her, the process was smooth and respectful, and I could rest easy knowing that my fair share of the proceeds would be securely and directly deposited into my account.

It was more than just paperwork—it was protection. It was friendship in action. Jean's support during this time reminded me that true friends don't just show up when it's easy. They stand beside you when the stakes are high and the ground feels unsteady. Her efforts lightened my burden in ways words could never fully express, and for that, I will always carry a deep, enduring gratitude in my heart.

As life settled into a more peaceful rhythm, I decided to mark a milestone—my 50th birthday—with something truly special: a trip to the United States to visit my daughters. After everything we had all been through, this felt like a well-deserved celebration, not just of age, but of resilience, love, and new beginnings.

From the moment I arrived, I was embraced not only by their arms but by the comfort of being seen, understood, and cherished. The scenery was breathtaking, from tree-lined streets to glowing city lights, but it was the laughter we shared, the late-night chats, and the quiet moments of simply being together that etched themselves into my heart.

We indulged in delicious meals, shopped for new outfits that felt like a fresh start, and made memories I'll carry with me forever. I felt pampered, uplifted, and—perhaps most importantly—young at heart again. Those three weeks were more than a vacation; they were a reunion of souls, a reminder that no matter how far we travel or how hard life gets, the bond between a mother and her daughters is unbreakable.

Returning home, I carried not just new clothes in my suitcase, but a heart full of gratitude, love, and renewed strength. It was the perfect way to step into a new decade of my life—with joy, connection, and a deep sense of hope for the future.

Chapter 22:

In 2018, I said goodbye to someone who had become more than just a friend—Jean was a guiding light during some of the darkest chapters of my life. Visiting her in palliative care was one of the hardest things I've ever done, yet it was also a sacred moment, a chance to express the deep gratitude I held for all the love, support, and wisdom she had so freely given over the years.

As I sat beside her, holding her hand, I thanked her—not just with words, but with my presence, my tears, and the quiet silence we shared. She had looked out for me when I couldn't look out for myself, fought for me when I didn't have the strength, and believed in me when I struggled to believe in anything at all.

Jean's passing left a tender ache in my heart, but also a deep, enduring warmth. Her kindness, generosity, and strength live on in the choices I make and the compassion I strive to offer others. She was the kind of friend who comes into your life like a gift—one you never forget, and always carry with you.

Around this time, I was blessed with one of life's most profound joys—I met my first grandchild. Holding that tiny bundle of life in my arms, I felt a love so immediate and overwhelming it brought tears to my eyes. In that moment, everything came full circle. It wasn't just about witnessing the next generation—it was about feeling the pulse of legacy, love, and hope beating in my arms.

Soon after, life gave me another precious gift. After five long years apart, my daughters moved back to Australia. Our reunion was nothing short of magical. We had weathered storms across oceans and time zones, but standing together again, I felt whole. The laughter, the hugs, even the simple shared moments like cooking together or walking side by side—all became treasures I held close.

Watching my daughters settle into their new lives—each in a loving home, with husbands by their sides, and the beginnings of their own families—filled me with pride and peace. They were strong, grounded women now, creating the kind of nurturing environments I had always dreamed of for them.

This new chapter—of being a mother, a grandmother, and a witness to life's beautiful continuation—has been a deeply rewarding experience. It reminded me that even after years of struggle, love always finds its way home.

The first time I held my grandchild in my arms, time stood still.

There was a hush in the room, a quiet reverence that wrapped itself around us like a warm blanket. As I looked down at the tiny face nestled against me, so new to the world, so delicate and perfect, a wave of emotion swept through me—so vast and tender, it took my breath away. I traced their little fingers with mine, marvelled at their soft cheeks, and listened to the gentle rhythm of their breathing. It was as if the universe had placed its most precious gift in my arms.

In that moment, I wasn't just a grandmother—I was a witness to the continuation of love through generations. All the hardships, sacrifices, and heartbreak I had endured somehow made sense now. I had lived through storms, and here I was, holding the calm—pure, innocent, and filled with possibility.

My heart felt fuller than it had in years. This child carried not just a new name, but the legacy of resilience, hope, and unconditional love. I saw pieces of my daughters in that tiny face, and in a quiet, overwhelming way, I saw myself too. That small heartbeat against my chest felt like the beginning of something beautiful and eternal.

It was more than a moment—it was a blessing; one I will carry with me for the rest of my life.

Grant and I built a solid, enduring foundation of friendship over the nine years I lived in his home. What began as a simple rental arrangement grew into something far more meaningful—he became not just a generous landlord, but a trusted confidant and a steady, grounding presence in my life.

Grant had a quiet wisdom about him, and his calm, thoughtful nature made it easy to open up. He never judged, never imposed—just listened with patience and spoke with sincerity. During some of my most challenging moments, his guidance and encouragement were like a gentle hand on my back, reminding me that I wasn't alone.

His belief in me, especially when my own confidence wavered, gave me the strength to keep moving forward. Whether it was through small conversations over tea, or his consistent, respectful support of my independence, Grant reminded me of the power of genuine friendship. In a world that had sometimes felt unpredictable and unkind, his presence was a quiet reassurance—proof that good people still existed, and that true friendship could be a source of healing.

The bond we formed over those years wasn't defined by grand gestures, but by everyday kindness and shared humanity. I will always hold deep gratitude for the role he played in my life—not just as someone who offered me a roof over my head, but as someone who helped me rebuild my sense of home within myself.

Now, I am embracing a new and hopeful chapter of my life. I've settled into an over-50s retirement village, just a short distance from my daughters and four beautiful grandchildren. Being close to them brings me an incredible sense of joy and completeness. The village itself has become more than just a place to live—it's a true community. The warmth, connection, and camaraderie I've found here have brought immense happiness and greatly improved my overall well-being.

I continue to focus on my physical health with regular physiotherapy and hydrotherapy. Despite the challenges of a permanent disability, I remain committed to achieving as much independence as possible. Using an ankle-foot orthotic (AFO) has been a game-changer. It's not just a medical device—it's a symbol of my determination to keep moving forward. It allows me to walk with more confidence and safety, especially in managing the effects of foot drop. While the functionality of my left hand remains limited, I stay proactive in maintaining movement and preventing further stiffness. These daily efforts are reminders of my resilience and the importance of adapting to life's evolving challenges.

During my time living with Grant, I also found purpose and connection through volunteering at a local nursing home for three years. It was one of the most heart-opening experiences of my life. Being able to sit beside residents, share stories, offer comfort, and simply be present taught me the deep value of compassion and kindness. Knowing that my presence made a small but meaningful difference in their lives filled me with a renewed sense of purpose. The smiles, the shared laughs, the quiet moments of understanding—those became some of the most treasured memories in my journey of healing.

Chapter 23:

Scars of the past couldn't silence the whispers of my heart. Even after everything I had endured, some quiet part of me still believed in love.

Both of my marriages had ended in betrayal—painful, unexpected heartbreaks that left me questioning everything I once believed about trust, partnership, and loyalty. The man I once called my husband had broken promises that were meant to last a lifetime. Twice. And with each betrayal, a piece of me shattered. I gave my heart fully, only to have it bruised by lies and deception. The wounds ran deep, leaving me guarded, uncertain, and weary.

For a long time, I shut love out. I told myself it was safer that way. That I had enough to carry on my own without the risk of being let down again. But deep down, I never truly gave up on love. I just tucked that hope away, keeping it safe while I healed.

It took time—and tremendous courage—but eventually, I allowed myself to hope again. To believe that not all love ends in pain. That somewhere out there, someone was waiting for a woman like me: strong, kind, wiser from the journey, and still open to giving her heart.

Through this challenging time, I learned that my story was far from over. My life in Australia was still unfolding, and though it had taken a painful turn, I was determined to find my way forward. The journey would be difficult, filled with ups and downs, but I knew that I had already overcome so much. I had the strength to rise above, to build a new life grounded in love, resilience, and the belief that even after betrayal, there is always the possibility of healing and new beginnings. A journey that was solely my own.

As I close this chapter of my story, I'm filled with gratitude for the incredible people who have supported me. To Grant, my amazing friend, landlord, and mentor—thank you for your unwavering kindness and wisdom. To my daughters—thank you for coming back to Australia and bringing joy back into my life. To Debbie—thank you for believing in my story and encouraging me to share it. As I look to the future, I am excited to see what lies ahead. I hope my story inspires others to stay strong, keep pushing forward, and never give up on their dreams.